SOUTHERN

Cooking

SOUTHERN

Cooking

MARJIE LAMBERT

CHARTWELL
BOOKS, INC.

A QUINTET BOOK

Published by Chartwell Books
A Division of Book Sales, Inc.
114 Northfield Avenue
Edison, New Jersey, 08837

This edition produced for sale
in the U.S.A., its territories
and dependencies only.

ISBN 0–7858–0025–5

Reprinted in 1994, 2004

This book was designed and produced by
Quintet Publishing Limited
6 Blundell Street
London N7 9BH

Creative Director: Richard Dewing
Designer: Fiona Akehurst
Project Editor: Stefanie Foster
Editor: Lisa Cussans
Photographer: Andrew Sydenham
Illustrator: Paul Collicut
Home Economists: Nicole Szabason and
Deborah Greatrex

DEDICATION
To my dad, who made me believe I could do
anything

ACKNOWLEDGEMENTS
With thanks to Laura and Stefanie at Quintet,
and, as always, to Terry

Typeset in Great Britain by
Central Southern Typesetters, Eastbourne
Manufactured in Singapore by
Eray Scan Pte Ltd
Printed in Singapore by
Star Standard Industries (Pte) Ltd

★ *PICTURE CREDITS* ★

Quintet Publishing would like to extend thanks to the following for providing location shots:
p6 Louisiana Office of Tourism; *p7* Arkansas Department of Parks and Tourism; *p8, 12, 14*
Louisiana Office of Tourism; *p24* Southern Carolina Division of Tourism; *p26* Virginia
Division of Tourism; *p33* Georgia Industry, Trade and Tourism; *p38, 52, 54, 64, 66* Louisiana
Office of Tourism; *p74* Arkansas Department of Parks and Tourism; *p78, 80, 90* Louisiana
Office of Tourism; *p97* Florida Department of Commerce, Division of Tourism; *p102*
Louisiana Office of Tourism; *p105* Kentucky Department of Travel Development; *p107*
Florida Department of Commerce, Division of Tourism; *p109* Southern Carolina Department
of Parks, Recreation and Tourism; *p121* Florida Department of Commerce, Division of
Tourism; *p142* Southern Carolina Department of Parks, Recreation and Tourism.

CONTENTS

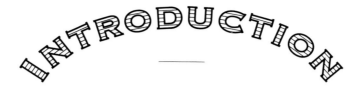

INTRODUCTION

Eating Southern food is like taking a shortcut back through the history of the South, for through its food, we can trace the South's family tree. It is a complex cuisine, because the tree has many branches. Traced to its roots, Southern cooking is the melding of three cultures — Native American, western European, and African. To a lesser extent, it is influenced by Mexican and Caribbean cuisines.

★ *ABOVE Drawing upon their heritage of folk songs from the British Isles, Southerners have made fiddling part of their traditions, as in this Louisiana fiddle contest.*

The many regional variations we see throughout the South are the branching out of different combinations of cultures and native foods. The spicy, often fiery, dishes of southern Louisiana are contributions of Cajuns and Creoles, who brought their French heritage to the mix. In Florida, Caribbean spices and produce add a different twist. The fisherman's bounty from the saltwater marshes of the Carolina Low Country is a mainstay of that area's cuisine. In Maryland and Virginia, seafood from the Chesapeake and refined plantation cooking are the dominant influences. Farther inland, in Kentucky and Tennessee, pioneer farmers who struggled to live off the land relied on simple but substantial meals of farm products.

But throughout the South, there is a shared foundation of common staples, the two most basic being pork and corn. Pork — brought to the South by European settlers — is pervasive in Southern cooking, from the famed Southern smoked ham, pork chops and roasts, to bacon, homemade sausage, salt pork, ham hocks, cracklings, and of course, pork fat. Many Southern dishes are cooked in pork fat or seasoned with pork. It has been only as health concerns have arisen in recent years that cooks have grudgingly used smaller amounts or substituted other products like vegetable oil.

Corn, which was a staple of Native American diets for thousands of years, is used in countless ways in Southern cooking. Fresh corn is fried, baked into pudding, mixed into salads, and stirred into soups and stews. Cornmeal is baked into dozens of variations of cornbread. And grits are

★ *ABOVE The elegant Short-Biere House in Helena,
Arkansas, is on The Great River Road along the Mississippi
River, just upstream of its junction with the Arkansas River.*

the most distinctly Southern food, though only because grits are underrated and unfairly scorned outside the South.

Other essential elements of the Southern kitchen hail from Africa — okra, peanuts, and yams, the last having largely been replaced by the American sweet potato. The tradition of long, slow cooking and one-pot meals are other African influences that contribute to dishes like gumbo.

Food is inextricably bound up in Southern culture. The South's legendary hospitality is based on the deep-rooted belief that it is a moral obligation to feed one's guests. For centuries after Europeans settled in the South, life centered around the production, preparation, and consumption of food. The social life of a community often revolved around meals, as well.

One of the legends of Southern cooking is its bounty — the groaning tables loaded with tremendous varieties of food. In the past, Southern meals often featured three or four vegetable dishes, breads and biscuits, a couple of starches, several kinds of pickles, and two or three pies and cakes, in addition to the main course. But that bounty is based on several

periods in Southern history when survival was a struggle. During the early years of European immigration and again during the Civil War era, food was scarce. African slaves often lived on what they could grow in their own gardens, small allotments of staples like cornmeal, as well as discards from the plantation kitchens like chicken necks, ham hocks, pigs feet, and entrails, or chitterlings.

From scarcity and poverty came a forced creativity with whatever ingredients were available. In this way evolved such standards as black-eyed peas seasoned with ham hocks; greens boiled with salt pork; cornbreads and corncakes made with only cornmeal, water, salt, and lard; and soups and stews based on chicken necks and pork scraps. The food that northerners refer to as soul food is those dishes and others, like chitterlings and sweet potato pie, that came out of slave kitchens. Sausage is made from the parts of pigs that would have otherwise gone to waste. Barbecuing — not grilling — is a way to tenderize tough, gristle-filled cuts like pork shoulder and spareribs. Catfish and crawfish were once scorned by all but the poor.

Southerners lived through hard winters by relying on the food they preserved in the smokehouse, by pickling and drying, and by canning summer produce. Generations after refrigeration became common, those traditions of other preservation methods continue to have a strong influence on Southern cuisine. True Southern smoked ham is rare and expensive, and is considered a gourmet item. Southerners continue to pickle foods that others would never think of pickling: pork, shrimp, peaches, watermelon rind. Homemade jams and jellies are made from the fruits of Southern orchards and vineyards, and served with the South's famed biscuits and breads.

Urbanization, airline travel, and television have all had an impact on Southern cuisine. Not only has Southern cooking spread outside the South, but other cultures continue to influence Southern cooking. *Nouvelle cuisine* items like goat cheese and sun-dried tomatoes are produced on Southern farms. Southern Junior League cookbooks are laced with recipes that call for non-Southern techniques and ingredients like stir-frying, soy sauce, tortillas, and salmon.

This cookbook attempts to combine the traditions of Southern cooking with the influences of the 1990s. Much traditional southern

★ *ABOVE In Covington, Louisiana, across Lake*
Pontchartrain from New Orleans, history buffs re-enact a
Civil War battle.

food is either fried or makes heavy use of fat or sugar. We have not eliminated those foods; you'll find recipes here for fried chicken, sausage balls, cream soups, pork chops and gravy, turnips and peas in cream sauce, fried potato patties, and a variety of Southern breads and sugary desserts. But we've tried to trim the fat in some traditional dishes like gumbo, and offered tasty alternatives like baked catfish and oven-fried chicken, grilled shrimp and chicken, and vegetables that are baked or grilled rather than fried. You'll also find some variations on Southern standards, like fried chicken that has been marinated in citrus juices, pear cobbler instead of peach, and fried oysters incorporated into a salad.

Suggested Menus

Luncheon 1

Butternut squash soup

Oyster salad

French bread

Ginger pear cobbler

Luncheon 2

Cream of watercress soup

Green salad

Vidalia onion pie

Buttermilk pie with

raspberry sauce

Brunch

Blackberry-molasses muffins

Ham frittata

Fried apples and pears

Pecan squares

Boiled cookies

Derby Day Brunch

Mint juleps

Shrimp butter and crackers

Asparagus-mushroom salad

Baked tomatoes

Burgoo

Country ham

Sweet potato biscuits

Kentucky jam cake

Picnic

Olive salad with crackers

Black-eyed pea salad

Assorted fresh fruits

Mini potato salads

Citrus-fried chicken

Jeannie's sheet cake

Summer Barbecue

Chicken skewers

Corn and kidney bean salad

Grilled Vidalia onions

Barbecued pork shoulder

Sandwich buns

Coconut cake

Dinner

Ham puffs

Strawberry-spinach salad

Mint-grilled sea bass

Baked cheese grits

Minted peas

Rhubarb custard pie

Cold Weather Dinner

Mushroom cups

Carrot-turnip soup

Roast pork with rhubarb sauce

Green bean bundles

Spicy rice stuffing with greens

Caramel apple pie

Watching Your Waist-line Dinner

Black-eyed pea dip with crudites

Gaspacho aspic

Spicy shark kabobs

Green beans and new potatoes in pesto

Strawberries in meringue nests

(without custard sauce)

INGREDIENTS

The delicious and varied character of Southern cooking comes from its creative melding of ingredients and cooking techniques from various cultures. European settlers brought farm livestock, including swine and chicken. Africans brought field peas, yams, okra, and peanuts. Native Americans grew corn and pumpkins. From coastal waters, rivers, and inland lakes came shrimp, crab, oysters, flounder, catfish, and a wealth of other fish and seafood. Farmers grew rice, and eventually learned they could farm crawfish in the same flooded fields. Many greens grew wild. On farms and in backyard gardens, Southerners cultivated squash, tomatoes, beans to be dried and others to be eaten fresh, eggplant, cucumbers, peppers, and other vegetables. Orchards and vines produced peaches, plums, pears, apples, blackberries, grapes, and other fruits in abundance, as well as pecans, almonds, and the now hard-to-find black walnuts and hickory nuts. Herbs and spices were used generously, whether they were native items like bay leaves and filé powder (ground sassafras) or brought in by other cultures, such as chile peppers and spices from Latin America and the Caribbean.

PORK

Pig farmers like to say they use every part of the pig except the squeal, and that's certainly true in Southern cooking.

The most celebrated cut of pork is the Southern ham, which is salt-cured, smoked, and dried to produce a lean, salty, smokey and dry meat. A true Southern ham must be scrubbed, soaked and boiled, but the result is delicious. However, true Southern-style hams are becoming more difficult and expensive to find. Modern hams are more likely to be soaked or injected with a brine of salt, sugar, chemicals, and maybe some artificial smoke flavoring, producing a meat that is not nearly as lean or smoky.

Bacon is critical to Southern cooking. In addition to enjoying fried bacon for its own sake, Southerners use it to flavor all kinds of dishes from cornbread to stewed vegetables, and they cook many foods in bacon fat.

Smoked ham hocks are used to flavor soups, stews, greens, and dried beans. Sausage is the featured ingredient in many Southern dishes, and some Southerners still make homemade sausage of pork scraps, herbs, spices, and salt. Pigs feet and chitterlings are staples of soul food.

CORN

Three staples of Southern cooking are simply corn in different forms: fresh; dried and ground into cornmeal; or dried and ground into grits and boiled.

Fresh corn is an ingredient in soups, stews, and salads. Sometimes frozen corn may be substituted for fresh. But in some recipes, like corn pudding, the milk from the corn is essential. After cutting the corn from the cob, scrape the cob with a dull knife to squeeze out the milk.

Southerners use cornmeal the way the rest of the country uses wheat flour. Even with those recipes that require the rising qualities of wheat flour, Southerners often throw in some cornmeal for texture, such as with cornmeal bread. Although Southerners traditionally prefer white cornmeal, there is not much difference between the white and yellow cornmeal available in grocery stores. The greater difference is between mass-produced, pre-packaged cornmeal, and fresh, stone-ground cornmeal. Although the fresh, stone-ground cornmeal has a better texture and flavor, it does not keep as well because it also contains more corn oil.

Grits are another, coarser form of ground corn. Grits are boiled long and slow for 30 minutes to an hour, then served with breakfast. But just because they are served plain doesn't mean they are eaten plain. Grits are used to mop up bits of egg and sausage or bacon. Basic boiled grits are also the foundation of other Southern dishes. They can be mixed with cheese, milk, butter and eggs, then baked in a casserole. They can be chilled, sliced, then grilled or baked with cheese. They can be used,

like rice or noodles, as the base for a thick meat sauce. Many grocery stores sell quick grits or instant grits. Purists disdain instant grits. However, quick grits, which are steamed and compressed to fracture the grains and take only five minutes to cook, are acceptable if you cook them 5–10 minutes longer than the time recommended on the package, tasting them to see when they've lost their raw flavor.

FISH AND SEAFOOD

Fish and seafood are integral parts of Southern cuisine. On the Chesapeake Bay, crabcakes are a staple. In the Carolinas, seafood boil – a combination of shellfish, spices, corn, sausage, and occasionally potatoes – is popular. Florida, which lies between the Atlantic and the Gulf of Mexico, has an abundance of fish and seafood popular in other states, as well as some, like conch, that aren't found elsewhere in the U.S.

Oysters of several varieties are found in Southern coastal states. Different varieties, Southern or not, can be used interchangeably in most recipes. Although some people worry about the effect of ocean contaminants, many oyster-lovers still eat the shellfish raw with a splash of hot sauce. Oysters are also eaten fried, in casseroles, soups, and stews. Look for oysters whose shells are still tightly closed, or freshly shucked oysters that are plump, have a creamy color, and are surrounded by clear liquid.

Like oysters, *crabs* are available in many varieties. Stone, blue-claw, and buster crabs are among those native to Southern states, and others are available in other parts of the country. Because their sizes vary widely, whole crabs can't be used interchangeably without adjusting for size. One Dungeness crab may have as much meat as six blue crabs. However, ounce for ounce of meat, one type of crab can be substituted for another. Use fresh crabmeat whenever possible, as canned meat does not have the same excellent flavor.

Shrimp are widely available and can increasingly be found for reasonable prices. Fresh shrimp is best, but may be hard to find since shrimpers often quick-freeze their catch right on board the boat. Frozen shrimp can be – but is not necessarily – mushy and flavorless. Seek out a good fish market. Shrimp comes in a wide range of sizes, the bigger, the more expensive. It is graded by the number of shrimp per pound. Most recipes in this cookbook call for medium to large shrimp, which means 12–40 shrimp per pound.

Catfish are widely farmed by commercial operations, some outside the South, although they are still often regarded as Southern. The most popular catfish dish is breaded, fried, and served with hushpuppies, but it can also be grilled, baked, poached, or cooked in a variety of other ways. It is a white-fleshed, firm-textured, medium-oily fish. In addition to plain fillets, many stores now sell catfish fillets with a spicy "Cajun" seasoning.

Pompano is the South's gourmet fish, delicate and expensive. It is excellent baked, steamed, or grilled. Substitute whole trout, flounder fillets, or red snapper if you cannot find pompano.

Trout is a common and popular fish found in Southern lakes and rivers as well as most of the rest of the country. One half-pound whole trout is the perfect serving size for one person. Serve it pan-fried, grilled, or baked. Speckled, rainbow, brown, and golden trout can be used interchangeably.

Shark steak, a less expensive alternative to the popular swordfish, is a firm, meaty fish that is delicious grilled or on kabobs.

Other fish commonly used in Southern cooking are *red snapper*, a low-fat, firm-textured fish that is adaptable to many recipes including blackened fish; *redfish*, the original blackened fish, which became so popular that the state of Louisiana temporarily banned its sale in order to save it; *grouper* and *sea bass*, which are both low-fat, firm-textured fish that are sometimes sold interchangeably; and *flounder* or *sole*, a low-fat, fine-textured fish.

★ *ABOVE Speckled trout from Louisiana are popular with fisherman and delicious to eat.*

DRIED BEANS AND PEAS

Southern cuisine makes wide use of dried beans and peas. Black-eyed peas, sometimes called field peas, are most widely recognized as a distinctly Southern ingredient. They are the main ingredient in Hopping John, a black-eyed peas and rice dish traditionally cooked on New Year's Day to bring good luck throughout the year.

SWEET POTATOES

Sweet potatoes, native to the U.S., are often confused with the yam, an African tuber, but no matter, since they are cooked the same way. The cooked pulp of sweet potatoes is used in pies, bread, soufflés, and other dishes. The potato can also be sliced and fried. Some people like them just roasted and buttered.

However, many other dried beans are popular in Southern cooking, including kidney beans, black or turtle beans, white beans, and lima beans. Often they are cooked with ham hocks or bacon for flavor. Not all dried beans have to be soaked overnight any more. Many can be boiled for a few minutes, then allowed to sit in the hot water for an hour. Check the package for directions.

APPETIZERS

Olive salad

Mushroom cups

Shrimp butter

Ham puffs

Chicken skewers

Sausage-stuffed mushrooms

Black-eyed pea dip

Sausage balls

Pickled shrimp

Crab roulade

Curried chicken salad in puffs

★ **OPPOSITE** *The sun sets over a Louisiana bayou.*

Olive Salad

MAKES ABOUT 3 CUPS

10 oz. green (Spanish) olives

3 oz. black olives

3 cloves garlic, finely minced

1 tbsp. chopped capers

⅓ cup chopped red onion

1 stalk celery, chopped

2 tbsp. olive oil

1 tbsp. red wine vinegar

1 tbsp. chopped fresh basil, or
*   1 tsp. dried*

2 tsp. chopped fresh oregano, or
*   ½ tsp. dried*

¼ tsp. pepper

Olive salad is a staple in New Orleans, where it is the star ingredient in that city's famed muffaletta sandwich and a legacy of the large population of Italian immigrants who settled there more than a century ago. Muffaletta sandwiches are made on large white buns with Italian meats and cheeses like salami and provolone. For hors d'oeuvres, consider stuffing meat, cheese, and olive salad into pita pockets, then cutting them into wedges. Or simply serve the olive salad as a chunky dip with crackers. For variety, add a few anchovies or some pine nuts to the olive salad.

Drain the green olives, reserving 2 tbsp. of the brine. Coarsely chop the olives. Drain the black olives, discard the brine, and coarsely chop. Add the garlic, capers, red onion and celery, and mix well.

Make a dressing by combining 2 tbsp. of the green olive brine with the remaining ingredients. Shake or whisk to combine, then pour over the salad and stir in.

Note: if you buy green olives that are not stuffed with pimento, add 2 tbsp. chopped sweet red pepper to the salad.

Mushroom Cups

MAKES 24 APPETIZERS

SHELLS

24 slices soft white bread

4 tbsp. butter, melted

¼ tsp. paprika

Crisp bread shells are filled with a sour cream and mushroom mixture for a hot hors d'oeuvre. The shells and filling for this appetizer can be made up to 24 hours in advance, then reheated just before serving.

Preheat oven to 400°F. With a cookie cutter or glass, cut a 2½-inch circle from each slice of bread. (Save the bread scraps to make breadcrumbs.) Mix the melted butter and paprika. Lightly butter the cups of two mini-muffin tins. Gently press a circle of bread into each cup. Using a pastry brush, lightly brush the inside of each bread cup with the remaining melted butter. You don't have to cover every spot or saturate the bread with butter. Bake at 400°F until the bread is crisp, 8–10 minutes.

To make the filling preheat oven to 350°F. Sauté the garlic, mushrooms, and green onions in the melted butter for 10 minutes. Sprinkle the flour, salt, pepper, and cayenne over the mushrooms, stir well, and cook 1 minute. Add the sherry. Stir and cook until the sherry evaporates, about 1 minute. Remove from heat and stir in the sour cream. Divide the filling among the bread shells. Bake 10 minutes if the filling is hot, 15 minutes if it has been made in advance and refrigerated.

FILLING

3 tbsp. butter

2 cloves garlic, minced

1 lb. mushrooms, coarsely chopped

½ cup chopped green onions

1 tbsp. flour

½ tsp. salt

¼ tsp. pepper

⅛ tsp. cayenne

2 tbsp. sherry

⅓ cup sour cream

Shrimp Butter

MAKES ABOUT 1½ CUPS

½ lb. cooked and cleaned shrimp,
  any size
½ cup butter at room
  temperature
2 tbsp. finely minced green onion
1 tsp. capers, drained
2 tsp. fresh lemon juice
½ tsp. grated horseradish
¼ tsp. salt
⅛ tsp. cayenne
dash of pepper

This easy hors d'oeuvre spread can be made ahead of time and brought to room temperature just before serving. Spread the shrimp butter on crackers or miniature toasts.

Put all ingredients in blender or food processor and process until smooth.

Ham Puffs

These savory puffs begin with cream-puff pastry, but change character dramatically with the addition of ham, cheese, green onion, and spices. They can be made ahead of time to the point of baking, and refrigerated on baking sheets, then popped in the oven at the last minute. If there are any leftovers — and that's doubtful — they can be frozen and reheated later.

Preheat oven to 400°F.

In a medium saucepan, bring water and butter to a boil. Mix the salt and spices with the flour, and add the flour to the pan, stirring until it forms a solid ball. Add the eggs, one at a time, stirring until each is incorporated into the mixture. Remove from heat. Add ¾ cup of the cheese, the ham and green onions. Stir well.

Divide dough into walnut-sized balls and place on baking sheets. Sprinkle remaining ¼ cup cheese over tops. Bake at 400°F until puffs are golden brown, 20–25 minutes. If the puffs were made in advance and refrigerated, cooking time will increase by 5–10 minutes.

MAKES ABOUT 30 PUFFS

6 tbsp. butter
1 cup water
1 cup all-purpose flour
½ tsp. salt
¼ tsp. pepper
½ tsp. dry mustard
¼ tsp. cayenne
4 eggs
1 cup grated Swiss cheese,
  divided
⅓ cup minced ham
3 tbsp. minced green onions

Chicken Skewers

MAKES 8 APPETIZER SERVINGS

4 boneless chicken half-breasts

½ cup olive oil

1 tbsp. fresh lime juice

2 tbsp. red wine vinegar

2 cloves garlic, minced

¼ tsp. cayenne

¼ tsp. black pepper

1 tbsp. chopped fresh basil, or 1 tsp. dried

1 tbsp. chopped fresh oregano, or 1 tsp. dried

Simple to make, these chicken skewers are marinated, then grilled on the barbecue. They can be served hot or cold, and are excellent finger foods for picnics and barbecues.

Cut the chicken into 4–5 strips each. Combine the remaining ingredients to make the marinade. Put the chicken in a shallow glass or other non-reactive dish. Pour the marinade over the chicken, and turn it to be sure all pieces are coated. Marinate the chicken in the refrigerator for at least 5 hours.

About 40 minutes before serving time, start a fire in the barbecue. If you are using wooden skewers, soak them in water for 30 minutes to avoid burning them.

Thread the chicken onto the skewers so they form an S-curve. Do not crowd the chicken, as it will not cook evenly. If the skewers are long, you may put two strips of chicken on each. When the flames have died and the coals are glowing, place the skewers on the grill over the coals. Turn the skewers at least once so both sides are cooked. Cooking time will be 10–15 minutes.

Sausage-Stuffed Mushrooms

MAKES 6 SERVINGS

24 large mushrooms
½ lb. sweet Italian sausage
olive oil, as needed
⅓ cup chopped onion
⅓ cup finely chopped celery
⅓ cup finely chopped green
 pepper
1 clove garlic, minced
¼ tsp. cayenne
¼ tsp. cumin
½ tsp. salt
¼ tsp. black pepper
6 tbsp. breadcrumbs
2–3 tbsp. milk, cream, or beef or
 chicken stock
Parmesan cheese

This appetizer will be a big hit. This recipe is only mildly spicy, but you can experiment with different types of sausage. You can stuff the mushrooms ahead of time, then keep them in the refrigerator until just before it's time to eat. If the mushrooms are cold, cooking time will increase a few minutes.

Preheat oven to 400°F.

Wipe mushroom caps clean with a damp cloth. Remove stems. Chop stems and reserve 1 cup for this recipe.

Remove casings from sausage. Crumble sausage into a skillet and sauté gently, adding a little olive oil if necessary, until meat is browned. Remove sausage with a slotted spoon and set aside.

Sauté chopped mushroom stems, onion, celery, green pepper and garlic in remaining fat, or add olive oil if needed. Cook until vegetables are tender, about 5 minutes. Add seasonings and mix well. Add breadcrumbs, sausage, and liquid. Mixture should be moist, but it won't adhere into a ball.

Lightly coat tops of mushroom caps with olive oil. Stuff caps with sausage mixture. Sprinkle with Parmesan cheese. Place mushrooms, stuffed side up, in shallow baking pan. Bake at 400°F until cheese is browned and mushrooms are tender, about 15 minutes.

Black-Eyed Pea Dip

Ham, crunchy vegetables, and liberal use of Tabasco sauce turn the humble black-eyed pea into a tasty dip. If you're a fan of spicy food, add finely chopped jalapeño pepper to the recipe. The dip is traditionally served with sesame crackers, but it's good with vegetable crudites, too.

Soak peas overnight. Drain. Place in medium saucepan with ham hocks, onion, and dried pepper. Add enough water to cover. Bring to a boil, then simmer until peas are tender, about 1 hour, adding water if needed. Drain the peas, reserving about ½ cup liquid and the ham hocks. Discard the onion and dried pepper.

Purée the peas in a blender or food processor, adding the cooking liquid a tablespoon at a time, until the mixture is still a little dry but almost smooth, probably 4–6 tbsp. Add the sour cream. Cut the meat from the ham hocks, discard the fatty parts, and mince the meat. Add it to the purée with the salt and black pepper. Just before serving, add the onion, green or red pepper, and Tabasco sauce to taste.

MAKES ABOUT 3 CUPS

1 cup dried black-eyed peas
1 large or 2 small ham hocks
1 medium onion, cut into chunks
1 dried red pepper
1 cup sour cream
1 tsp. salt
¼ tsp. black pepper
⅓ cup chopped green onion
⅓ cup chopped green or sweet
 red pepper
Tabasco sauce, to taste

Sausage Balls

MAKES ABOUT 30 APPETIZERS

12 oz. spicy pork sausage
1 cup grated cheddar cheese
1 cup all-purpose flour
2 tsp. baking powder
½ cup chopped red onion
3 tbsp. milk

Sausage balls are easy to make, and you can vary them by using different types of sausage. Serve them with toothpicks and a bowl of good mustard for dipping.

Preheat oven to 350°F.

Crumble the sausage into a bowl. Add the remaining ingredients and knead them together. Shape the mixture into balls. You can make them to this point and refrigerate them until shortly before serving time. Place the sausage balls in a shallow baking pan and bake them at 350°F until browned, 15–20 minutes. Drain briefly on paper towels, and serve them while they're still hot.

Pickled Shrimp

2 lb. medium or large shrimp
1 lemon, halved
2 dried red chiles
1 tbsp. whole mustard seed
1 tsp. black peppercorns
1 tbsp. whole coriander seed
marinade (recipe follows)

MARINADE
1½ cups white wine vinegar
¾ cup good-quality olive oil
2 tbsp. Dijon-style mustard
1 onion, thinly sliced
1 lemon, seeded and thinly sliced
1 tbsp. whole mustard seed
1 tbsp. whole coriander seed
1½ tsp. red pepper flakes
3 garlic cloves, minced
½ tsp. salt

Pickled shrimp should be made at least 8 hours before you plan to serve it, but it's even better if you make it the night before. Set it out in a pretty dish, with toothpicks for serving.

Bring a large pot of water to a boil. Add lemon, chiles, and spices. Boil for at least 20 minutes to develop flavor. While the water is boiling, peel and devein the shrimp. Add the shrimp to the water and cook just until the shrimp turn an opaque white-pink and curl tightly, 2–3 minutes, depending on their size. Do not overcook or the shrimp will be tough. Drain the shrimp and plunge them into cold water to stop the cooking. Drain well. Put the shrimp in a glass or other non-reactive bowl. Pour the marinade over them and turn the shrimp so all are coated. Refrigerate at least 8 hours or up to 24 hours, stirring occasionally.

To make the marinade whisk together the oil, vinegar, and mustard. Stir in remaining ingredients and mix well.

Crab Roulade

MAKES 30–40 HORS D'OUEVRES

ROULADE

2 tbsp. butter

4 tbsp. flour

¼ tsp. salt

1 cup hot milk

4 eggs, separated

2 tbsp. minced chives

CRAB SPREAD

3 oz. cream cheese

1–2 tbsp. milk

2 green onions, minced

1 tsp. fresh lemon juice

1 tsp. capers, drained and
    chopped

⅛ tsp. cayenne

4 oz. fresh crabmeat

This elegant hors d'oeuvre is made by spreading a rich crab filling over very thin sponge dough, rolling it into a cylinder, and slicing it into pinwheels. It is not difficult to make, and can be assembled in advance. The roulade showcases the flavor of crab, so use fresh crabmeat.

Preheat oven to 375°F. Line a 10 × 15-inch jellyroll pan or baking sheet with parchment paper. Butter the paper.

Melt 2 tbsp. butter in a small saucepan. Whisk in the flour and salt, then the hot milk. Continue cooking and whisking until the mixture is thick and smooth. Remove from heat. Add a tablespoonful of the hot mixture to the egg yolks and whisk. Add several more spoonfuls, one at a time, then pour the yolk mixture into the pan with the remaining milk mixture. Add chives. Whisk until smooth.

In a medium bowl, beat the egg whites until soft peaks form. Gently fold into the hot batter.

Spread the batter evenly over the buttered parchment. Bake at 375°F until the roulade is lightly browned, 15–20 minutes. Don't worry if it cracks or puffs up. Pierce any puffy spots with a knifetip. The roulade will "heal" itself as it cools.

When the roulade is cool, cover it with a clean towel and turn it upside down so it sits on the towel. Carefully peel off the parchment. Cut the roulade in half across its width. Gently spread the crab spread thinly across the surface of both rectangles, going to the very edge. Starting with the cut edge, roll each roulade into a

tight cylinder, so you have two 7½-inch rolls. There should be enough crab spread at the end of the roulade that the edge of the dough sticks to the cylinder. Note: The recipe may be prepared up to this point a day in advance. Don't slice the roulade more than a couple of hours in advance or it may dry out. Slice the roulade into thin pinwheels of about ⅓–½ inch each. Arrange on a plate, and refrigerate until serving time.

To make the crab spread, in a small bowl, thin the cream cheese with the milk until it has the consistency of soft butter. It must not be runny. Add the green onions, lemon juice, capers and cayenne, and mix well. Pick over the crabmeat with your fingers to remove any bits of shell or cartilage. Stir the crabmeat into the cream cheese mixture.

Curried Chicken Salad in Puffs

MAKES 24–30 SMALL PUFFS

PUFFS

1 cup milk
⅓ cup butter
dash of salt
1 cup all-purpose flour
4 eggs at room temperature

CURRIED CHICKEN
SALAD

2 cups cooked chicken, slivered
1 large or 2 small peaches, peeled and cubed
½ cup small seedless grapes
¼ cup slivered almonds
2 tbsp. chopped green onions
¼ cup chopped celery
⅓ cup mayonnaise
⅓ cup sour cream
2 tsp. curry powder
¼ tsp. salt

Too many people are intimidated by cream puff shells. They are really not that daunting. Here, they're filled with chicken salad for delicious hors d'oeuvres or picnic finger food. Try other savory fillings, such as crab or ham salad. The puffs and salad can be made early in the day, then assembled about an hour before serving.

Preheat the oven to 400°F. Cover two baking sheets with foil or waxed paper, and lightly grease the paper.

Bring the milk, butter, and salt to a boil in a medium saucepan. Add in all the flour at once. Stir constantly until the mixture turns into a thick dough that pulls away from the sides of the pan. Remove from heat. Add one egg at a time, beating the dough with a wooden spoon until each egg is fully incorporated before adding the next.

Using a spoon or a pastry bag, form the dough into walnut-sized balls. Place the balls on the cookie sheets. Bake for

10 minutes at 400°F, then reduce the heat to 350°F and bake until the puffs are golden brown, about 25 minutes. Cool away from any drafts. When the puffs are cool, slice off the tops with a sharp knife. Remove any damp dough filaments from inside. Fill with chicken salad and replace the tops. Keep filled puffs refrigerated until serving time.

Now to the salad. If the peaches are very juicy, set them in a colander to drain while you mix the other ingredients. Or go ahead and put them in the salad; you'll just have a juicier salad.

Combine the chicken, peaches, grapes, almonds, onions, and celery in a medium bowl. In a separate bowl, mix the mayonnaise, sour cream, curry powder, and salt. Add the dressing to the salad and mix thoroughly. If the salad seems dry, add a little mayonnaise.

To avoid soggy puffs, fill the puffs with the salad no more than 1 hour before serving time.

★ *ABOVE America's oldest landscaped gardens, created by slaves over a 10-year period, are at Middleton Place, an Ashley River plantation near Charlestown, South Carolina.*

SALADS

Fried chicken salad

Asparagus-mushroom salad

Strawberry-spinach salad

Cucumber salad

Warm pasta salad

Corn and kidney bean salad

Black-eyed pea salad

Mini potato salads

Oyster salad

Gazpacho aspic

Peach salsa

Shrimp-melon salad

★ **OPPOSITE** *Virginia's stunning fall foliage, seen at Wintergreen, a ski resort in the Blue Ridge Mountains.*

Fried Chicken Salad

MAKES 2 SERVINGS

CHICKEN

2 half chicken breasts, boneless

1/3 cup flour

1/4 tsp. salt

1/2 tsp. paprika

1/4 tsp. black pepper

1/4 tsp. dried thyme

1/8 tsp. celery salt

oil for frying

Make salad into a main dish with the addition of warm strips of fried chicken. For ease of cooking and slicing, use boneless chicken breasts. Top with your favorite buttermilk-style dressing.

Mix flour and seasonings. Dredge chicken breasts in seasoned flour. Heat 1/4-inch oil in skillet. When it's hot but not smoking, carefully add chicken. Fry over medium heat, turning once, until outside is crispy and no pink is visible when you cut into the chicken, 10–15 minutes, depending on the thickness of the chicken.

Let the chicken cool slightly. While it is cooling, divide the lettuce, mushrooms, celery, green onion, and olives between two plates. Cut the chicken into strips and arrange strips on top of salad. Serve with a buttermilk-style dressing.

SALAD

chicken strips

3–4 cups torn lettuce leaves, any type

1/2 cup sliced mushrooms

1 stalk celery, diced

1 green onion, chopped

pitted black olives

Asparagus-Mushroom Salad

MAKES 4 SERVINGS

1¹/₂ lb. fresh asparagus

¹/₄ lb. mushrooms

2 tbsp. white wine vinegar

¹/₂ cup olive oil

¹/₄ tsp. Dijon-style mustard

*1 garlic clove, crushed in garlic
    press*

¹/₄ tsp. fresh chives

*¹/₄ tsp. fresh thyme, or a dash of
    dried thyme*

*¹/₄ tsp. fresh oregano, or a dash of
    dried oregano*

¹/₄ tsp. salt

dash of pepper

In Kentucky, asparagus is a traditional part of Derby Day brunch, and here's one way to serve it. The combination of asparagus and mushrooms makes a sophisticated salad. Just be sure that you give the asparagus a head start on the vinaigrette: mushrooms are notorious sponges, and will soak up the dressing before the asparagus has a chance to absorb any of the flavor.

Snap bottoms off asparagus spears. Blanch 3–5 minutes in boiling water, depending on thickness of spears. Drain and chill.

Prepare the vinaigrette by mixing all the remaining ingredients except the mushrooms. Shake well and pour over asparagus.

After the asparagus has been in the vinaigrette at least 20 minutes, clean, trim, and slice the mushrooms. Add them to the salad, and spoon some of the vinaigrette over them. Allow to marinate at least another 20 minutes.

Strawberry-Spinach Salad

SALAD

4 cups Bibb lettuce, cleaned and
   torn into bite-size pieces
4 cups spinach, cleaned and torn
   into bite-size pieces
2 cups whole strawberries,
   washed and hulled
1/3 cup chopped celery
2 tbsp. chopped fresh chives
1/3 cup pecan pieces
2 avocados, peeled and cubed

Sweet and tangy strawberries complement creamy avocado in this spring green salad. The dressing is a surprisingly delicious blend of flavors, including strawberries, basil, garlic, chives, honey, and mustard.

Divide the lettuce and spinach among six bowls. Top with the strawberries, celery, chives, pecans, and avocado.

Combine all the dressing ingredients and mix well, preferably in a blender or food processor.

DRESSING

4 large, hulled strawberries,
   puréed
1/2 cup vegetable oil
2 tbsp. white wine vinegar
1 tbsp. chopped fresh basil, or 1
   tsp. dried
1 tbsp. chopped fresh chives
1 garlic clove, finely minced
1/4 tsp. prepared mustard
1 tsp. honey
1/4 tsp. salt
1/4 tsp. freshly ground pepper

Cucumber Salad

MAKES 4 SERVINGS

2 large cucumbers, peeled and
    thinly sliced
1/2 Vidalia or other sweet onion,
    thinly sliced
1/2 sweet red pepper, cut into
    julienne strips
1/3 cup olive oil
2 tbsp. fresh lemon juice
1 garlic clove, pressed
2 tsp. minced fresh parsley
1 tsp. minced fresh tarragon
1/4 tsp. salt
dash of freshly ground pepper

You can use cucumbers from the grocery store if you wish, but the ones from your garden will work just as well. This salad benefits from a couple hours of marinating.

Put the cucumbers, onions, and pepper in bowl. Make dressing by combining the remaining ingredients, then whisk or shake well. Pour the dressing over the salad.

Warm Pasta Salad

MAKES 4 SERVINGS

8 oz. fusilli or other pasta

6 stalks asparagus

3 tbsp. extra-virgin olive oil

1/3 cup fresh grated Parmesan
    cheese, plus extra for topping

1/2 small zucchini, thinly sliced

2 green onions, chopped

1/2 cup walnut pieces

1/3 cup green olives, quartered

salt and pepper to taste

This salad combines the saltiness of green olives, the crunch of walnuts, and the goodness of fresh vegetables. Use fresh grated Parmesan cheese, not the packaged kind; you'll notice a big difference in flavor. The flavors are enhanced when this salad is served warm, but if you have any cold leftovers, add a splash of vinaigrette for flavor.

Cook pasta according to directions on package. While the pasta is cooking, blanch the asparagus for 2–3 minutes in boiling water. Drain asparagus, and cut into 1-inch pieces.

When the pasta is cooked, drain but do not rinse, then put it in a large mixing bowl. Pour olive oil over pasta, and toss with two forks. Add the Parmesan, and toss again. Stir in the asparagus, zucchini, green onions, walnuts, and green olives. Add salt and pepper to taste. Serve with a sprinkling of Parmesan over the top.

Corn and Kidney Bean Salad

MAKES 6 SERVINGS

3 cups fresh corn

15-oz. can kidney beans, rinsed
and drained

1/2 cup diced sweet red pepper

1/2 cup diced green pepper

1/2 cup chopped green onion

2 large tomatoes, seeded and
chopped

1/4 cup chopped fresh cilantro

1/3 cup olive oil

1/3 cup fresh lime juice

1 clove garlic, minced

1 tsp. ground cumin

1/4 tsp. cayenne

1/2 tsp. salt

1/4 tsp. black pepper

optional: 1 jalapeno pepper,
seeded and finely minced

Fresh vegetables and kidney beans combine for a spicy, crunchy salad that is easy to make. It's also delicious used as a topping with grilled chicken or fish. For added flavor, roast the corn on the grill instead of cooking it on the stovetop. And for a spicier salad, add a jalapeno pepper.

Cook the corn, either by roasting it on the cob, or cutting it off the cob and boiling it in its own juice and a scant amount of water for about 5 minutes. Drain corn and let it cool while you mix the other ingredients.

In a large bowl, mix kidney beans, red and green peppers, green onions, tomatoes, cilantro, and jalapeno if desired. Add the corn when it's cool.

In a small jar, mix the remaining ingredients. Shake well and pour over salad. The salad benefits if you prepare it several hours in advance and allow the flavors to mix.

Black-eyed Pea Salad

MAKES 8-10 SERVINGS

3 1-lb. cans of black-eyed peas,
rinsed and drained

2 cups red onion, chopped

1 cup chopped green pepper

1 jalapeno pepper, seeded and
finely chopped

1/4 cup chopped fresh cilantro

3 cloves garlic, finely minced

1/2 cup olive oil

1/2 cup red wine vinegar

1 tsp. brown sugar

1 tsp. salt

1/4 tsp. black pepper

few drops Tabasco sauce

Black-eyed peas are mixed with onions and peppers and marinated in oil and vinegar for a variation of a dish that is sometimes called Dixie caviar. Although this recipe calls for a single jalapeno pepper to make a mildly spicy dish, some people use 3–4 peppers. The salad tastes best after it has marinated at least 24 hours. It makes an excellent accompaniment to barbecue.

Mix the black-eyed peas, onion, green and jalapeno peppers, cilantro and garlic. Make a dressing of the remaining ingredients and shake or whisk so they are well mixed. Pour over the salad. Just before serving, taste and adjust salt and Tabasco sauce to taste.

★ *ABOVE Cotton farming was responsible for much of the white settlement of the Deep South. As plantation owners exhausted farmlands trying to supply England's hungry cotton mills, they moved further south and established new plantations.*

Mini Potato Salads

20 small (not tiny) new potatoes, 1½–2 lb.

1 large or 2 small green onions, finely minced

1 hard-boiled egg, chopped

⅓ cup sour cream

3 tbsp. mayonnaise

2 tbsp. chopped fresh dill

¼ tsp. salt

dash of black pepper

Talk about convenience! These bite-sized potato cups are perfect finger food for a picnic or barbecue. Hollow out small new potatoes, use the pulp for potato salad, and stuff the potato shells with the salad. Although some people may politely stop with 1–2, it's easy to eat 6–8 of these. This salad has a Scandinavian influence with the dill and sour cream.

Scrub but don't peel the potatoes. Put them in a pot of boiling water and cook until they are tender, 12–18 minutes, depending on their size. Drain the potatoes and let them cool.

Cut the cool potatoes in half. With a melon baller, scoop out the pulp, but leave a shell of about ⅛-inch. Chop the pulp. Add the green onion, egg, sour cream, mayonnaise, dill, salt, and pepper. If it will be more than a couple of hours before you eat, don't stuff the potatoes yet. The salad may dry a little and need the addition of a little sour cream or mayonnaise just before stuffing.

Mound the stuffing into the potato shells. Garnish with a sprig of dill, if desired.

Oyster Salad

Deep-fried oysters are served on a salad of mixed greens with Vidalia sweet onions, peaches, and Asiago cheese. Gulf and Louisiana oysters are particularly popular in the South, but use any fresh oyster in this salad. The salad greens include bitter greens such as mustard or dandelion mixed in for a flavor contrast. Corn flour is available in many natural-food stores, but you can substitute more cornmeal for the corn flour.

Clean the greens, and tear them into bite-size pieces. Separate the onion slices into rings. Peel the peaches, and cut them into chunks. Divide the greens, onions, and peaches among four plates. Put four fried oysters on each salad. Sprinkle with Asiago cheese. Use the dressing on page 30 (dressing for Cucumber Salad) or other favorite vinaigrette.

To make the fried oysters combine the cornmeal, corn flour, and seasonings. Dip the oysters in the cornmeal mixture. In a deep skillet or wok, heat oil to 365°F. With tongs, drop in several oysters at a time, but don't crowd them; they should not touch during cooking. Cook until golden brown, turning once, about 3 minutes. Drain well on paper towels. Make sure oil has returned to 365°F before cooking next batch. Keep fried oysters warm in oven while you are frying remaining oysters.

1 bunch spinach, arugula, or Bibb lettuce

1 bunch dandelion or mustard greens, or two heads endive

several thick slices Vidalia or other sweet onion

1 large or 2 small ripe peaches

Asiago cheese

16 fried oysters (recipe follows)

FRIED OYSTERS

16 medium to large fresh oysters, shucked

⅔ cup cornmeal

⅓ cup corn flour

½ tsp. salt

¼ tsp. black pepper

¼ tsp. cayenne

vegetable oil for frying

Gazpacho Aspic

MAKES 6 SERVINGS

1 cup ripe tomatoes, seeded and chopped

³/4 cup minced green pepper, divided

1/2 cup seeded and diced cucumber, divided

2 chopped green onions, green and white parts separated

2 tsp. chopped fresh cilantro

2 tsp. chopped fresh basil

1 clove garlic, minced

2 envelopes unflavored gelatin

1¹/2 cups canned tomato juice

1 cup chicken stock

³/4 cup finely diced celery

1 tsp. salt

1/2 tsp. Worcestershire sauce

few drops Tabasco sauce

Gazpacho aspic is a cool way to eat your vegetables on a hot day. Raid the garden for fresh vegetables, and make this aspic early in the day. Some of the vegetables are puréed, and some are added in their chopped form to make a chunky aspic. Like gazpacho soup, you can spice it up with extra Tabasco if you like your food spicy. The aspic is good plain, but you can also dress it up with a little herbed mayonnaise.

Purée the tomatoes, ¹/4 cup of the green pepper, ¹/4 cup of the cucumber, the white part of the green onions, cilantro, basil, and garlic. Set aside.

Pour ¹/2 cup of the tomato juice into a small bowl and sprinkle the gelatin over it. While the gelatin is dissolving, heat the remaining tomato juice, chicken stock, and purée in a medium saucepan. If the gelatin begins to set, put some water in a shallow pan and set the bowl in the pan. The water should not come near the top of the bowl. Put the pan over low heat. The gelatin will dissolve. Add the mixture to the aspic mixture and bring it to a boil. Remove from heat and add the celery, vegetables, salt, Worcestershire, and Tabasco.

Pour into a 4-cup mold or bowl. Refrigerate at least 4 hours, or until set.

Peach Salsa

MAKES ABOUT 1½ CUPS

4 ripe peaches, peeled and
    chopped
⅓ cup chopped green onion
2 jalapeño chiles, seeded and
    finely chopped
¼ cup sweet red pepper, chopped
2 tbsp. chopped fresh cilantro
3 tbsp. fresh lime juice
¼ tsp. chili powder
salt and pepper to taste

Peaches and chiles seem like an odd combination, but they make a delicious topping for grilled seafood or chicken. This recipe is moderately spicy but not hot. If you like hot food, leave some of the jalapeño seeds in. This salsa can be made up a day in advance, but it does not keep well beyond that.

Mash about ¼ of the peaches to make a juicy base. Stir in the rest of the peaches and the remaining ingredients. Let sit about 15 minutes, then taste and adjust seasonings.

Shrimp-Melon Salad

Bibb lettuce from Kentucky, shrimp from the coastal waters, and cantaloupe from Southern farms make a light and tasty summer salad, topped with a slightly sweet dressing.

Toss the shrimp with the lime juice and let them sit, refrigerated, about 30 minutes before preparing the salad.

    Divide lettuce among four plates. Add shrimp, melon, and green onions. Pour dressing over each salad and serve.

MAKES 4 SERVINGS

1 lb. medium or large shrimp,
    cooked and cleaned
2–3 tbsp. fresh lime juice
4–5 cups Bibb lettuce, washed
    and torn into bite-size pieces
2 cups cantaloupe balls
2 green onions, chopped

DRESSING

½ cup olive or other vegetable oil
4 tbsp. lime juice
1 tbsp. honey
2 tsp. finely chopped chives
1 tsp. Dijon-style mustard
dash of salt and pepper

Shrimp-Melon Salad

SOUPS & STEWS

Ham and corn chowder

Butternut squash soup

Gumbo

Burgoo

Cabbage, bean, and ham soup

Frogmore stew

Pumpkin soup

Shrimp-artichoke soup

Carrot-turnip soup

Cream of watercress soup

Black bean soup

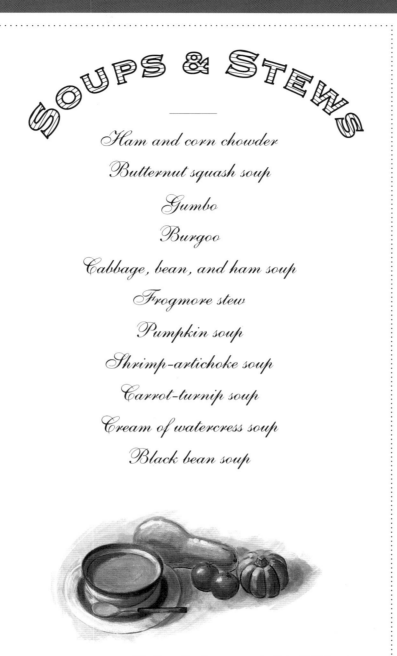

★ **OPPOSITE** *The Pontalba Apartments, built in 1850 by the Baroness Almonester Pontalba, are reputed to be the oldest apartments in the United States. The Pontalba Apartments sit on Jackson Square in New Orleans.*

Ham and Corn Chowder

MAKES 4–6 SERVINGS

2 ham hocks (about 1½ lb.)

*1 medium onion, peeled and
    quartered*

*2 stalks celery, cut into 3-inch
    pieces*

2 carrots, cut into 3-inch pieces

several sprigs of fresh parsley

1 bay leaf

3 cups chicken broth

3 cups corn (4–5 ears)

½ tsp. cumin

⅛ tsp. cayenne

⅛ tsp. white pepper

1 cup heavy cream

½ cup chopped green onions

¼ cup chopped sweet red pepper

Ham and corn are such integral parts of Southern cuisine that we combined them in this inexpensive corn chowder. Use fresh corn if it's available, or frozen if not. The last-minute addition of green onions and red peppers adds crunch and color.

Place the ham hocks, onion, celery, carrots, parsley, and bay leaf in a large pan, and cover with water. Bring to a boil and simmer about 1½ hours. Remove the ham hocks, and cut off the meat. Return the bones to the pot, and continue reducing the broth. Cut the ham meat into slivers.

Strain the ham broth and discard the vegetables. Combine 1 cup of the ham broth in a large saucepan with 3 cups chicken broth. Bring to a boil. Add the corn, the slivered ham and the spices, and simmer for 20 minutes. Add cream, green onions and red peppers, and bring just barely to the boiling point. Taste and adjust for seasoning. The ham is salty and should provide enough salt.

Butternut Squash Soup

MAKES 4–6 SERVINGS

2 medium butternut squash
  (approximately 3 lb.)
1–2 tbsp. olive oil
3 tbsp. butter
2 leeks (about 1½ lb.) chopped,
  white part only
3 cups chicken stock
¼ tsp. white pepper
½ tsp. dried oregano
½ tsp. dried thyme
1 cup buttermilk
salt to taste

This is a versatile soup: it can be made with different kinds of squashes, including acorn and zucchini, so you can enjoy it throughout the year, changing it to fit whatever is in season. The buttermilk adds a creamy, slightly tangy flavor rather than a sharp, identifiable buttermilk taste, so you don't have to be a buttermilk-lover to like it. However, if you really dislike buttermilk, you can substitute heavy cream. To save time, bake the squash the night before you plan to eat the soup.

Preheat oven to 350°F. Cut squash in half lengthwise, and brush flesh with olive oil. Bake until tender, about 45 minutes. Let cool slightly. Scoop out the pulp.

In a heavy saucepan, sauté the leeks in butter 10 minutes. Add the squash, stock, and seasonings. Bring to a boil and simmer 10 minutes. In two or three batches, purée the soup in a blender or food processor. Return the soup to the heat and bring to a boil. Add the buttermilk and heat, but do not let the soup boil. Add salt to taste.

Gumbo

MAKES 8 SERVINGS

2 whole or 4 half chicken breasts,
    skinned and cubed

2 tbsp. flour

1/2 tsp. salt

1/4 tsp. black pepper

1/4 tsp. cayenne pepper

1 tsp. paprika

1/2 tsp. onion powder

1/2 tsp. garlic powder

2 tbsp. oil

2 cups chopped onion

1 cup chopped green pepper

1 1/2 cups chopped celery

2 cloves garlic, minced

1/2 cup lard, shortening, or
    vegetable oil

1/2 cup flour

2 quarts chicken stock

3 medium tomatoes, seeded and
    chopped

3/4 lb. Andouille sausage or other
    spicy smoked sausage, sliced

3/4 lb. medium shrimp, peeled and
    deveined

1/2 cup chopped green onion

1/4 cup chopped fresh parsley

6 cups cooked rice

Gumbo is a spicy stew of meat and vegetables served over rice. It comes from New Orleans, where cooks include all kinds of meats, from oysters and frogs legs to duck and sausage. This recipe calls for a combination of chicken, shrimp and spicy smoked sausage, but you can make substitutions freely. It is a spicy but not quite fiery dish, seasoned by the spices in the sausage, and those that the chicken is cooked in. The stew can be thickened with okra, filé powder (powdered sassafras leaves), or roux, a heated mixture of fat and flour that adds color and a smoky flavor. Recognizing people's concerns about fat and their health, this recipe uses a smaller amount of roux than is traditional. Since roux can be temperamental, it's recommended that you read the instructions thoroughly before you begin cooking.

Mix 2 tbsp. flour with the salt and other seasonings. Sprinkle over the cubed chicken, and toss so the cubes are evenly coated. Heat 2 tbsp. oil in a skillet, and sauté the chicken until it is cooked through and lightly browned, 8–10 minutes. Refrigerate.

Have the chopped onion, pepper, celery, and garlic ready before you make the roux. Heat the lard, shortening, or oil in a medium saucepan. The pan should be a little oversized for the quantity you're cooking because the roux gets dangerously hot, and you will want the extra depth in case it splashes around.

When the fat is hot, add the flour and whisk it in until the mixture is smooth. Turn the heat to low. Continue cooking,

stirring constantly. The roux will turn ivory, then beige, then gradually darken through different shades of brown. Cook until the roux is darker than a golden-brown bread crust, but has not turned chocolate brown. This will take about 30 minutes over low heat. You must stir constantly to keep the roux from burning. If black flecks appear in the roux, discard it and start over. The burned flavor will permeate the gumbo and ruin it. Never taste or touch the roux, and use extreme caution while stirring. Its temperature can reach 500°F.

When the roux reaches a medium brown, remove it from the heat. It will continue darkening, even away from the heat source. The way to stop the cooking is to add the chopped vegetables. Gradually and carefully stir in the vegetables until they are coated with roux. Then return the roux to the stove, and cook until vegetables are limp, about 5 minutes. Remove from heat.

In a large pot, bring 2 quarts of chicken stock to a boil. Add a few spoonfuls to the roux and stir, then add the roux to the stock. Add the cooked chicken, tomatoes, and sausage. Simmer uncovered for 20 minutes, stirring occasionally. If the sausage is fatty, you may need to skim fat off the top of the gumbo. Taste and adjust seasonings.

Just before serving, add the shrimp to the gumbo and cook until shrimp turns white-pink and tightly curled, 2–3 minutes. Stir in the green onions and parsley, and serve in bowls over rice.

Burgoo

MAKES 10–12 SERVINGS

2–3 lb. lamb's breast
3 lb. pork shoulder
1–2 lb. beef shank or soup bones
2 onions, quartered
3 carrots, cut into chunks
3 stalks celery, cut into chunks
several sprigs of parsley
2 bay leaves
stewing chicken, 3–4 lb.
1½ cups chopped onion
3 carrots, peeled and diced
1 cup chopped celery
2 cups potatoes, peeled and diced
1½ cups lima beans
2 cups tomatoes, seeded and
   chopped
2 cups corn
1 cup sliced okra
1 tsp. dried thyme
½ tsp. oregano
½ tsp. black pepper
½ tsp. cayenne
1 tsp. Worcestershire sauce
2 tsp. salt
2–4 tbsp. bourbon, optional
1 cup chopped parsley

Burgoo is a hunters' stew from Kentucky. It began as a long-simmering stew that featured game—squirrel, rabbit, venison, or whatever else could be found—and seasonal vegetables. Traditionally, it includes at least one type of red meat and one type of fowl, plus corn, tomatoes, lima beans, okra, and onion. Typically, it is also highly seasoned, although that doesn't necessarily mean hot. Curry, bourbon, filé powder (powdered sassafras leaves), and chile peppers are all possibilities. That leaves room for a great deal of variety. This version of burgoo features bony, inexpensive cuts of meat that are simmered for hours to create a thick, rich stew. If you start this stew a day in advance, you'll have time to chill the broth overnight and skim off the fat, and to let the meat cool before you separate it from the bones and fat, and chop it for the stew. If the biggest pot you have is an 8-quart stockpot, you'll need extra time to cook the meat first, remove, then cook the chicken.

Put the lamb, pork, beef, quartered onions, carrots, celery, parsley, and bay leaves in a big stockpot, and add enough water to cover by a couple of inches. Bring the water to a boil and skim off any scum that rises to the surface. Simmer for about 1 hour, then add the chicken. Again, scoop off any scum. Simmer for at least 90 minutes. You will need 2 quarts of broth for the stew, measured after the fat has been removed, so add water during cooking if necessary to be sure you're left with at least that amount.

Note: If you are working with a small stockpot, simmer the red meats for 2½–3½ hours, until the meat is tender and falling off the bone. Remove the meat, add the chicken, and simmer for 90 minutes.

Remove big items from the soup and strain it. Pour the broth into shallow pans or bowls and chill. Discard the cooked vegetables. Chill the meat if you have time. Trim the meat from the fat and bones, and chop or shred it into bite-size pieces. Do the same with the chicken. Skim the fat from the top of the broth.

Return the broth and the chopped meat to the stockpot, and bring to a boil. (If you've come up with less than 2 quarts of stock, supplement it with canned chicken or beef stock.) Add the chopped onion, carrots, celery, potatoes, lima beans and tomatoes, and simmer, covered, for 30 minutes. Add the corn, okra, thyme, oregano, pepper, cayenne, and Worcestershire sauce. Simmer 15 minutes. Add the bourbon, if desired, during the last 5 minutes of cooking, and the salt. Taste and adjust salt and cayenne. Just before serving, stir in the parsley.

Cabbage, Bean, and Ham Soup

MAKES 6 SERVINGS

1 cup dried lima beans

1 tbsp. olive oil

1 cup chopped onion

3 cloves garlic, minced

2 carrots, peeled and chopped

6 cups chicken stock

2 cups water

2 cups diced ham

2 sprigs of parsley

2 bay leaves

1 tsp. fresh thyme, or ¹/₄ tsp. dried

¹/₄ tsp. dried sage

3 cups shredded green cabbage

salt and pepper to taste

Serve this hearty winter soup with cornmeal bread and cheese.

Put lima beans in a large saucepan. Add 1 quart of water. Bring water to a boil, boil for 2 minutes. Remove pan from heat, and let beans soak for 1 hour in the hot water. Drain the beans.

In a small skillet, sauté onion, garlic, and carrots in olive oil for 5 minutes. Put the drained beans and the sautéed vegetables in the large saucepan with chicken stock, 2 cups water, ham, parsley, bay leaves, thyme, and sage. Simmer, uncovered, until the beans are tender, about 1 hour. Add the shredded cabbage. Cook until the cabbage is tender, about 5 minutes. Add salt and pepper to taste.

Frogmore Stew

MAKES 8 SERVINGS

4 bay leaves

1 tbsp. whole mustard seed

1 tbsp. whole coriander seed

1 tbsp. black peppercorns

1 tsp. whole cloves

1 tsp. celery seed

4 dried red chiles

4 cloves garlic, peeled and
  crushed

2 lemons, quartered

2 onions, quartered

8 ears corn, broken in half

2 lb. spicy smoked sausage, cut
  into ¾-inch lengths

3 lb. medium to large shrimp,
  unpeeled

This isn't really a stew, but a version of the seafood boil popular along the southeastern coast and particularly in the Low Country of the Carolinas. Frogmore doesn't have anything to do with frogs, but is the name of a small island community in South Carolina. This isn't a complicated dish, and can be varied easily. Some people prefer to cook their seafood in flat beer rather than water. Others vary the spices or use a commercial blend. New potatoes, clams, and crabs are popular additions. When the stew is done, drain off the water and arrange the ingredients on a huge platter. Serve with a good French bread, spicy cocktail sauce for the shrimp, and butter for the corn.

Fill a large stockpot one-half to two-thirds with water. Add the bay leaves and other seasonings, chiles, garlic, lemon, and onion. Bring the water to a boil and let it simmer about 20 minutes to develop the flavor.

Add the corn and cook 8 minutes. Add the sausage and shrimp. Cook until the sausage is warmed through and the shrimp is tightly curled and has turned an opaque pink-white, about 3 minutes. Drain off the water, and put the stew ingredients onto a huge platter.

Note: You may substitute uncooked sausage for the smoked sausage, but it must be cooked before you add it to the stew.

Pumpkin Soup

MAKES 6–8 SERVINGS

2 tbsp. butter or vegetable oil

1 cup chopped onion

⅓ cup diced carrot

⅓ cup chopped celery

2 cloves garlic, minced

4 cups chicken stock, divided

1 tsp. dried oregano, or 1 tbsp.
  fresh

2 tsp. ground cumin

¼ tsp. cayenne

2 lb. cooked pumpkin

½ cup sour cream

1 cup heavy cream

salt and pepper to taste

roasted seeds (recipe follows)

If you're using canned pumpkin, you can buy pumpkin seeds in the snack or Mexican-food section of many grocery stores. If you make the soup with fresh pumpkin, cut the pumpkin into cubes, scrape away the seeds and stringy pulp, and remove the tough outer skin. Then saute the cubes in butter over low heat until the pumpkin is tender. A 2½–3 lb. pumpkin yields 2 lb. cooked.

In a large, heavy pot, sauté onion, carrot, celery, and garlic in oil until soft, about 5 minutes. Add 1 cup chicken stock, oregano, cumin, cayenne, and pumpkin. Mix well. Bring to a boil, then lower heat and simmer, covered, for 20 minutes. Purée the pumpkin mixture in batches in a blender or food processor. Return purée to pan. Add remaining chicken stock and bring to a boil. Add sour cream and heavy cream, salt and pepper to taste. Heat but do not boil. Serve topped with roasted seeds.

To make the seeds, preheat oven to 400°F. Heat oil in small skillet. Add garlic and red chiles, and cook until garlic is lightly browned. Press the garlic and chiles to squeeze out juices, then remove from pan and discard. Add the cumin and paprika, stir well, and cook over low heat about 1 minute to develop flavor. Remove from heat. Add the pumpkin seeds and salt, and toss to coat evenly. Spread seeds in a single layer on a baking sheet. Toast in oven at 400°F for 5 minutes.

SEEDS

1 tbsp. olive oil

2 cloves garlic, peeled and
  crushed

2 dried red chiles

1 tsp. ground cumin

½ tsp. paprika

¼ cup shelled pumpkin seeds

¼ tsp. salt

Frogmore Stew

Shrimp-Artichoke Soup

MAKES 4–6 SERVINGS

3 artichokes

1 tbsp. fresh lemon juice

$\frac{1}{2}$ tsp. salt

2 tbsp. olive oil

2 garlic cloves, crushed

2 tbsp. butter

$\frac{1}{2}$ cup chopped onion

1 cup sliced mushrooms

1 clove garlic, minced

4 cups chicken broth

1 tsp. dried basil, or 1 tbsp. fresh

$\frac{1}{4}$ tsp. white pepper

$\frac{1}{2}$ lb. medium shrimp, peeled, deveined, and cut into bite-size pieces

1 cup heavy cream

dash of sherry, optional

salt to taste

Artichokes are popular in New Orleans and can be found throughout the South. They provide a delicate and delicious flavor that combines well with shrimp in this cream soup. Only fresh artichokes will do, since the water they were cooked in is a crucial part of the recipe.

Place the artichokes in a large pot. Add the lemon juice, salt, olive oil and crushed garlic cloves, and add enough water to cover by several inches. Boil the artichokes until they are tender, about 45 minutes depending on their size. Remove the artichokes, drain them by placing upside-down on paper towels, and let them sit until they are cool enough to touch. Continue to simmer the cooking liquid in order to reduce it. You will need 1$\frac{1}{2}$ cups.

Pull off the artichoke leaves, and scrape the tender meat at the base of each leaf into a bowl. Discard the leaves and the hairy choke. Cut the stem off the base, trim off the outer stringy portion, and chop the remaining part of the stem into the bowl with the leaf scrapings. Cut the artichoke hearts into chunks, and set aside in a separate bowl.

In a skillet, melt the butter and sauté the onion, mushrooms, and minced garlic.

In a large saucepan, bring to a boil the chicken broth and 1$\frac{1}{2}$ cups of the artichoke water. Add the onions and mushrooms, the artichoke scrapings (but not the chunks of artichoke heart), the basil and white pepper. Simmer, covered, for 15 minutes. Let the soup cool slightly, then purée it in batches in a blender or food processor.

Return the puréed soup to the stove, and bring to a boil. Add the shrimp and cook until they have turned an opaque pink-white, 2–3 minutes. Add the cream, artichoke hearts, the optional sherry, and salt, if needed. Bring barely to the boiling point, and serve.

Carrot-Turnip Soup

MAKES 4 SERVINGS

2 tbsp. olive oil or butter

1$\frac{1}{2}$ cups chopped onion

1$\frac{1}{2}$ lb. carrots, peeled and finely chopped (about 5 cups)

1 medium turnip, peeled and finely chopped

4 cups chicken stock

$\frac{1}{4}$ cup orange juice

1 tsp. ground ginger

$\frac{1}{4}$ tsp. nutmeg

salt and pepper to taste

Carrot and turnip are simmered in chicken stock, puréed into a thick broth, then seasoned with orange juice and ginger to make this soup. Serve it with a sandwich or salad for lunch, or as a first course at dinner.

Sauté the onions in oil or butter until the onions are golden, about 25 minutes. Put the onions in a large saucepan with the carrots, turnip, and chicken stock. Bring the mixture to a boil, reduce heat and simmer, uncovered, 40 minutes. Purée the soup in batches and return it to the heat. Add orange juice, ginger, and nutmeg. Bring to a boil, then reduce heat and simmer 5 minutes. Taste and add salt and pepper, and adjust ginger if desired.

Shrimp-Artichoke Soup

Cream of Watercress Soup

MAKES 4 SERVINGS

4 tbsp. butter

1½ cups chopped onions

½ cup chopped green onions

3 bunches watercress

3 cups chicken stock

1½ cups potato, cooked, peeled
and diced (about 1 lb.)

2 tsp. fresh lemon juice

1½ tsp. dried dill, or 1 tbsp. fresh

¼ tsp. white pepper

½ tsp. paprika

1 cup heavy cream

salt to taste

Watercress is a tasty, peppery green that grows wild along the creeks of the South. It brings a wonderful flavor to this rich cream soup.

Melt butter in heavy pot. Sauté onions and green onions over low heat until light gold, 20–25 minutes.

Meanwhile, clean watercress. Immerse in at least two baths of clean water and rinse well. Remove the leaves and tender stems, and discard the tough stems.

Add the watercress to the onions and sauté for 5 minutes. Add potato, 1 cup chicken stock, lemon juice, and dill. Simmer 5 minutes. Let cool slightly. Purée in batches in blender or food processor. Pour purée back into pot. Add remaining chicken stock, pepper, and paprika. Bring to a boil. Add cream. Warm until just barely at boiling point. Taste, and add salt if needed.

Black Bean Soup

MAKES 8 SERVINGS

2 cups dried black beans (about 1 lb.)

2 tbsp. vegetable oil

3 cups chopped onion

6 cloves garlic, minced

1 cup diced celery

8 cups chicken stock

ham bone or 1–2 smoked ham hocks

2 tsp. ground cumin

¼ tsp. cayenne

2 tsp. dried oregano

2 tsp. brown sugar

1 tbsp. fresh lime juice

½ sweet red pepper, chopped

2 tbsp. sherry

1 lb. Andouille sausage, sliced

sour cream

chopped green onion

chopped fresh cilantro

This is a hearty, spicy soup. This recipe calls for Andouille sausage, a very spicy smoked Louisiana sausage. You can substitute another sausage but be sure to leave time to cook it if it's an uncooked sausage. The soup is good without the sausage, too.

Pick through the dry beans for pebbles. Put the beans in a large pan, adding water several inches deeper than the beans. Put the pan on the stove, and bring the water to a boil. Remove from heat, and let the beans sit for 1 hour. Pour off the water, and rinse well.

In a skillet, sauté the onion, garlic, and celery in oil until vegetables are tender, about 5 minutes.

Return the beans to the pan. Add the chicken stock, sautéed vegetables, and ham bone or ham hocks. Bring the beans to a boil, reduce heat, and let the beans simmer, uncovered, for 1 hour.

Add cumin, cayenne, oregano, brown sugar, lime juice, red pepper, and sherry. Simmer the beans over low heat until they are tender, about 30 minutes longer. Add water or chicken stock if necessary, as the beans must not dry out, and there should be some excess liquid.

Purée the soup in batches in a blender or food processor.

Return the puree to the pot and reheat. Add the sausage, and simmer about 10 minutes longer. To serve, top each bowl with a dollop of sour cream, and garnish with cilantro and green onions.

BREADS

Cornbread

Blackberry cornbread

Sally Lunn bread

Pumpkin bread

Blueberry-cornmeal pancakes

Skillet cornbread

Baked pecan French toast

Spoon bread

Sweet potato biscuits

Blackberry-molasses muffins

Sweet potato bread or rolls

Cornmeal yeast bread

Moravian sugar bread

★ OPPOSITE *The Jungle Gardens at Avery Island,*
Louisiana, are filled with exotic plants, both native and imported.
The gardens are also a nesting spot for the snowy egret.

CORNBREAD

Early cornbread was a subsistence food, made of cornmeal, salt, lard, and water. Farmers put batter on hot hoes and cooked them in the coals of a fire, thus the name hoecakes. Similar patties cooked in the ashes of a fire were called ashcakes. Later, milk and eggs were added to the mix to make the oven-baked cornbread we know today.

Two basic styles of cornbread are popular today. The more traditional cornbread is coarse and crusty, made with little or no flour. Skillet cornbread (page 59) is an example of this style, although Southern purists disdain any flour or sugar in their cornbread. Skillet cornbread makes the perfect accompaniment to greens or black bean soup, and is an excellent base for stuffings. Another way of eating cornbread in the South is to crumble it into a cold glass of buttermilk. To make cracklin' bread, another popular variation, omit the sugar, substitute cornmeal for the flour, and add pork cracklings or crumbled bacon.

The other style is a very light, almost fluffy, sweet cornbread. A lot of sugar and a high proportion of flour to cornmeal make it more like cake than bread. Blackberry cornbread (opposite) is a nod to this style, although it is neither as sweet nor as fluffy as some popular recipes. Use it as a breakfast bread. It is not appropriate teamed with savory dishes.

Spoonbread (page 61) is considered by Southerners to be a more sophisticated evolution of cornbread. It is very moist, more like a pudding than a bread. It is served with a spoon and eaten with butter and jam, if desired, and it is traditionally served as a side dish.

★ *ABOVE The San Francisco, a Steamboat Gothic era house built in 1849 on the Mississippi River, west of New Orleans. The 22-room house features scrolls, fluted pillars and carved grillwork.*

Blackberry Cornbread

SERVES 4–6

1¼ cups all-purpose flour

¾ cup cornmeal

½ tsp. salt

2½ tsp. baking powder

½ cup sugar

2 eggs, lightly beaten

¾ cup milk

¼ cup butter, melted

2 cups blackberries, fresh or frozen

This cornbread is lighter and sweeter than the traditional Southern cornbread. The blackberries give it a purplish color and a wonderful flavor. It's delicious with blueberries or raspberries, too.

Preheat oven to 400°F. Lightly grease an 8 × 8-inch baking pan.

Sift dry ingredients together. In a separate bowl, combine eggs, milk and melted butter. Pour liquid ingredients into flour mixture, and stir well. Add berries and mix. Pour batter into baking pan. Bake at 400°F until top is lightly browned, about 30 minutes. Cut into squares and serve warm.

Sally Lunn Bread

1 package (about 1 tbsp.) dry
  yeast
1/2 cup water
1/3 cup sugar
1/2 cup butter, melted
1 cup milk
1 1/2 tsp. salt
3 eggs, lightly beaten with a fork
about 4 cups all-purpose flour

Sally Lunn bread is an elegant bread, baked in a tube pan like an angel food cake. Its texture somewhat resembles an angel food cake, too, airy and delicate. A good bread knife is needed, although James Beard recommended his Sally Lunn be torn apart with forks rather than cut. The bread is made with eggs, and the dough is too wet to be kneaded, so it is beaten with a wooden spoon.

Combine the yeast with the water – which must be between 100°–115°F – and the sugar in a large mixing bowl. Allow the yeast to ferment. After a few minutes, it will be foamy and there will be a few bubbles. If this doesn't happen, you need to start over. Either the yeast is too old, the water wasn't warm enough to activate the yeast, or it was so warm that it killed the yeast.

While the yeast is proofing, melt the butter. Allow it to cool slightly, and add it to the milk. Add the milk-butter mixture and the salt to the yeast mixture, and stir well. Add the eggs and stir well. Add the flour, a half-cup or so at a time, beating with a wooden spoon until it is well incorporated. When all the flour is mixed in, the dough should be a stiff batter. It will be too thick to pour easily, but too wet to knead. Continue beating another 100 strokes so that the dough is shiny and slightly sticky.

Cover the bowl with a clean cloth, set it in a warm place, and allow the dough to rise until it has doubled in bulk, 1–1 1/2 hours.

While the dough is rising, butter a 9-inch or 10-inch tube pan.

Beat the dough down with a wooden spoon, stirring for about a minute. Pour and scrape the mixture into the tube pan. Cover the pan with a cloth, and again set it in a warm place. Allow the dough to rise again until it has at least doubled in bulk, 1–1 1/2 hours.

Preheat oven to 375°F. Place the pan on a rack about one-third of the way up from the bottom. This is a tall bread, and you don't want the top to come too close to the upper heating elements.

Bake until top is golden brown, 35–45 minutes.

Pumpkin Bread

1²/₃ cups all-purpose flour
¼ tsp. baking powder
1 tsp. baking soda
¾ tsp. salt
½ tsp. cinnamon
¼ tsp. cloves
½ tsp. ginger
½ tsp. nutmeg
6 tbsp. butter
1¼ cups sugar
2 tbsp. molasses
2 eggs
1 cup cooked pumpkin
⅓ cup milk
½ cup pecans or walnuts
½ cup raisins

Moist and spicy, pumpkin bread is a delicious tea bread. Serve it with cream cheese flavored with a little strawberry jam or orange marmalade.

Preheat oven to 350°F. Grease a 9 × 5-inch loaf pan.
Mix dry ingredients in a large bowl.

In another bowl, cream the butter and sugar. Add molasses and eggs, and beat the mixture. Add pumpkin and milk and mix well. Pour the pumpkin mixture into the dry ingredients. Mix well. Stir in the nuts and raisins. Pour batter into a greased loaf pan. Bake until knife inserted in middle comes out clean, about 1 hour.

Blueberry-Cornmeal Pancakes

MAKES ABOUT 14 4-INCH CAKES

1 cup all-purpose flour

1/2 cup cornmeal

1 tsp. baking powder

1 tsp. baking soda

1 tsp. salt

1 tbsp. sugar

1 1/4–1 1/2 cups buttermilk

3 tbsp. melted butter

2 eggs

1 cup blueberries

oil for cooking

Cornmeal adds texture and a crispy finish to these pancakes. Use fresh blueberries if possible, or let frozen berries defrost and drain before mixing them into the batter. This recipe also makes good waffles with the addition of another 2 tbsp. butter.

Mix the dry ingredients. In a separate bowl, mix buttermilk, melted butter, and eggs. Pour the liquid ingredients into the dry ingredients. Stir just until the dry ingredients are moistened; don't worry about small lumps. The batter improves if it is prepared to this point and allowed to rest in the refrigerator overnight. Stir in the blueberries just before cooking.

Heat a slight amount of oil or use a frying pan with a soapstone finish. When the pan is hot, pour batter from a spoon held low over the pan. Cook 2–3 minutes, until bubbles form on top but don't break, then turn when underside is browned. Continue cooking about 2 minutes until browned on both sides (although second side will not be as evenly browned). Serve immediately or keep warm in oven.

Skillet Cornbread

SERVES 6–8

1½ cups cornmeal

½ cup all-purpose flour

1 tsp. salt

2 tsp. baking powder

1 tsp. baking soda

1 tbsp. sugar

3 eggs, lightly beaten

1½ cups buttermilk

6 tbsp. butter, melted

1 cup fresh-cut corn (1 large ear)
   or canned cream corn

1 tbsp. vegetable oil or bacon fat

This is a dense and hearty cornbread, baked in a hot skillet so that it has a crusty finish. Corn gives it added texture. Cut sweet, fresh corn right off the cob, or use canned cream corn. For variety, fry two or three strips of bacon in the skillet, then crumble the bacon into the batter and cook the cornbread in the hot bacon fat.

Preheat oven to 425°F.

Sift dry ingredients together. In a separate bowl, combine eggs, buttermilk and melted butter. Pour liquid ingredients into flour mixture and stir well. Add corn and mix.

Heat oil or fat in 9-inch or 10-inch cast-iron skillet, brushing some of the oil up the sides of the pan. When the pan is very hot and the oil is close to smoking, pour the batter in the pan. Immediately remove it from the burner and put it in the oven. Bake until golden brown on top, about 30 minutes. Cut into wedges and serve warm.

Baked Pecan French Toast

MAKES 4 SERVINGS

8 slices of stale bread, sliced ³/4-
   inch thick

8 eggs

1 cup milk

¹/2 cup light cream

¹/4 cup maple syrup

¹/3 cup brown sugar

¹/3 cup pecan pieces

Here's a way to fix French toast the night before, then just pop it in the oven in morning, freeing you to prepare other breakfast fixings while the French toast bakes. It's important to use dense, stale bread, like French or Italian bread, so that it doesn't turn mushy.

Put the bread in one large or two small lightly greased baking pans. The bread should not be so crowded that it is squished together. Beat together the eggs, milk, cream, and maple syrup. Pour the mixture over the bread. Turn the bread so it is coated on both sides with the egg mixture. Refrigerate overnight.

In the morning, preheat the oven to 350°F. Sprinkle the pecans, then the brown sugar, evenly over the bread. Bake until the bread is puffy and lightly browned, about 35 minutes.

Spoonbread

MAKES 6 SERVINGS

1 cup cornmeal

2 cups water

1 tsp. salt

3 tbsp. butter

1 cup milk

3 eggs, separated

Spoonbread is made with the same ingredients as cornbread, but in different proportions so that it has the consistency of pudding, lightened by the addition of beaten egg whites. It is too moist to be sliced; spoon individual servings out of the baking pan. Use it as a side dish, served with butter and, if you wish, jam.

Preheat oven to 375°F. Lightly grease an 9 × 9-inch baking pan.

In a medium saucepan, bring cornmeal, water, and salt to a boil. Cook over low heat for 5 minutes, stirring constantly. Remove from heat. Add butter and stir until butter is melted and blended. Gradually add milk and egg yolks, and mix well. Beat egg whites until soft peaks form Gently fold egg whites into cornmeal mixture.

Bake at 375°F until top is lightly browned, about 40 minutes.

Sweet Potato Biscuits

MAKES ABOUT 18 BISCUITS, DEPENDING ON SIZE

2 cups all-purpose flour

4 tsp. baking powder

1 tsp. salt

2 tsp. sugar

1/2 tsp. nutmeg

6 tbsp. butter or shortening

1 cup cooked, mashed sweet potato

1/3 cup milk

The addition of mashed sweet potato to a traditional biscuit dough makes the dough a little more difficult to handle, so we've chosen a drop biscuit instead of a rolled one. But the sweet potato gives the biscuits a lovely flavor. Serve them with butter and preserves — try apple butter — or make tiny sandwiches with thinly sliced ham.

Preheat oven to 450°F. Lightly grease two baking sheets.

Mix the dry ingredients. Cut in the shortening with two sharp knives, or work it in with your fingertips. Purée the sweet potato with the milk, and mix it into the dough.

Scoop out large, rounded tablespoons of dough and place them on the cookie sheets. Pat down any errant fingers of dough.

Bake at 450°F until barely browned, about 15 minutes.

Blackberry-Molasses Muffins

MAKES 9 LARGE MUFFINS

1¼ cups all-purpose flour

½ cup oat bran

½ tsp. baking soda

½ tsp. baking powder

¼ tsp salt

½ tsp. nutmeg

1 tsp. grated lemon peel

¼ cup sugar

2 tbsp. molasses

1 egg, beaten with a fork

¼ cup vegetable oil

½ cup buttermilk

1 tsp. vanilla

1–1½ cups blackberries, fresh or
  frozen

The blackberries that grow wild throughout the South inspired these muffins. The molasses adds a spicy sweetness, and the oat bran gives them an interesting texture. This recipe makes 9 large muffins, but you can produce more if you fill the tins half full or use smaller tins. The cooking time will be reduced, depending on the size of the muffins.

Preheat oven to 400°F. Lightly grease muffin tin.

Combine dry ingredients, lemon peel, and sugar. In a separate bowl, mix molasses, egg, oil, buttermilk, and vanilla. Pour milk mixture into dry ingredients and mix by hand, stirring only until ingredients are well incorporated. Stir in the blackberries. Divide batter among muffin tins. Bake at 400°F for 22–26 minutes.

Sweet Potato Bread or Rolls

MAKES 2 LOAVES OR 24 ROLLS

2 packages (about 2 tbsp.) dry
  yeast

½ cup water

¼ cup sugar

1 cup cooked and mashed sweet
  potato

1 cup plus 2 tbsp. milk, divided

1 tbsp. salt

¼ cup melted butter

about 5 cups all-purpose flour

1 egg

This is a moist, light-textured bread with a subtle flavor of sweet potatoes. It is equally good made into dinner rolls. For a slightly different flavor, add 1 tsp. nutmeg.

Dissolve the yeast and sugar in ½ cup water between 100°–115°F. While the yeast is proofing, mix sweet potato, 1 cup milk, salt, melted butter, and the nutmeg if desired, in a large mixing bowl. When the yeast has developed a foamy head, add it to the sweet potatoes and mix well. Stir in the flour, one cup at a time. When the dough is stiff, place it on a floured board and knead at least 5 minutes, continuing to add flour until the dough is very elastic and not sticky.

Put the dough in a large buttered bowl, and cover. Place in a warm, draft-free spot until dough has doubled in bulk, about 1 hour. Punch the dough down. Divide the dough between two buttered 9 × 5-inch loaf pans. Or cut off golf-ball-sized pieces of dough, pat them into balls, and put them into buttered muffin tins. Put the dough in a warm place, cover, and let it rise until it has once again doubled in bulk.

Bake in a preheated oven at 400°F, about 20 minutes for the rolls and about 35–40 minutes for loaves.

Make a glaze for the bread by beating together one egg and the remaining 2 tablespoons milk. Brush the glaze over the top of the loaves or rolls during the last 10 minutes of cooking.

Blackberry-Molasses Muffins

Cornmeal Yeast Bread

MAKES 2 LOAVES

2 cups water

3 tbsp. butter

2 tsp. salt

1 cup cornmeal

1 package (about 1 tbsp.) dry
yeast

¼ cup water

1 tbsp. sugar

1 cup milk

about 4 cups all-purpose flour

Cornmeal yeast bread, which begins with a cup of cornmeal cooked in boiling water, has a somewhat denser, chewier texture than plain white bread. It is wonderful sliced and toasted, or with cheese melted on top.

In a medium saucepan, bring the water, butter, and salt to a boil. Add the cornmeal and stir continuously as the meal absorbs the water and becomes a thick paste. Continue cooking, stirring all the while, for 1 minute. Remove the cornmeal from the heat, and put it in a large mixing bowl to cool.

After the cornmeal has cooled for a few minutes, proof the yeast. Dissolve the yeast and sugar in ¼ cup of water that is between 100°–115°F.

While the yeast is proofing, mix milk into cornmeal mixture. Work it in with your hands, checking for any lumps and working them out with your fingertips. After the yeast has developed a head of foam, add it to the cornmeal and stir it in. Add the flour, one cup at a time, stirring

well. After you've added the third cup, begin kneading it with your hands. When the dough is stiff enough to pull away from the side of the bowl, turn it onto a floured board and continue kneading at least 5 minutes, until the dough is very elastic and not sticky.

Butter a large bowl, and place the dough in it. Cover with a clean towel. Set the dough in a warm, draft-free place until it doubles in bulk, 1–1½ hours. Punch the dough down and divide it in half. Butter two 9 × 5-inch loaf pans. Roughly shape the dough into two loaf shapes, and pat into place in the pans. Again, cover the dough and put it in a warm, draft-free place until it has doubled in bulk.

Bake 10 minutes in an oven that has been preheated to 425°F, then lower oven temperature to 350°F. Bake about 25 minutes, or until bread is browned and sounds hollow when tapped. You may remove the loaves from the pans and put them back in the oven for a few minutes to crisp the crust.

★ *RIGHT Sam Houston Jones State Park in Lake Charles, western Louisiana. Lake Charles is a modern port once used by buccaneer Jean Lafitte.*

Moravian Sugar Bread

MAKES 2 LOAVES, WITH
9 SERVINGS EACH

1½ tbsp. (1½ packages) dry yeast

½ cup warm water

⅔ cup sugar, divided

½ cup butter, melted

¾ cup milk

⅔ cup mashed potatoes

1 tsp. salt

2 eggs

5–6 cups all-purpose flour

topping (recipe follows)

TOPPING

1 cup brown sugar

1 tsp. cinnamon

½ tsp. nutmeg

½ cup butter

Slightly sweet dough made with mashed potatoes and topped with butter and brown sugar is more like a coffee cake than bread. It comes from the 18th century Moravian settlements of North Carolina, and is traditionally associated with Christmas.

Dissolve the yeast and 2 tbsp. sugar in ½ cup warm water (between 100°–115°F). While the yeast is proofing, melt the butter and add it to the milk. When the yeast has developed a foamy head, add it to the milk. Mix in the mashed potatoes, remaining sugar, salt and eggs. Stir in the flour, a cup at a time, until dough is stiff. Knead it on a floured board 5 minutes or so, until dough is very elastic and has lost its stickiness.

Put the dough in a large oiled bowl. Cover and put in a warm place. Let the dough rise until it has doubled in bulk, 1–1½ hours. Punch the dough down. Divide it in half. Put the dough in two 9 × 9-inch square baking pans. Cover the pans and let the dough rise until it has again doubled in bulk.

Make the topping. Combine ingredients in a small saucepan. Heat, stirring often, until butter is melted and sugar dissolved. With your finger, gently make shallow indentations all over the tops of the two loaves. Spread the topping across the bread, letting it pool in the indentations. The topping will melt and spread during the baking, so it is not necessary that the bread be completely coated.

Bake the bread in a preheated oven at 375°F for 25–30 minutes. Cut into 9 squares like a tic-tac-toe grid.

VEGETABLES

Creole mixed vegetables

Minted peas

Corn pudding

Creamed turnips and peas

Sweet potato-apple soufflé

Roast corn

Fried corn

Grilled Vidalia onions

Vidalia onion pie

Green beans and new potatoes in pesto

Green bean bundles

Greens with dumplings

Baked tomatoes

★ *LEFT Raven Cliff Falls provides one of South Carolina's most spectacular views.*

Creole Mixed Vegetables

MAKES 6 SERVINGS

4 strips bacon

1 tbsp. bacon fat or vegetable oil

1 cup chopped onion

1/2 cup chopped green pepper

2 cups seeded and chopped
    tomatoes

1 cup sliced okra

1/2 tsp. salt

1/4 tsp. pepper

1/8 tsp. cayenne

1 tsp. sugar

2 cups corn

1 cup lima beans

Some of the South's favorite vegetables are featured in this colorful dish, which is finished with a scattering of bacon bits. You may use frozen corn, okra, and lima beans.

Fry bacon until it is crisp. Drain on paper towels.

In a large saucepan, in 1 tbsp. bacon fat or vegetable oil, sauté the onion and green pepper until they are tender, about 5 minutes. Add tomatoes, okra, salt, pepper, cayenne, and sugar. Bring to a boil, adding a few tablespoons of water if necessary. Lower heat and simmer, covered, 20 minutes. Check once or twice, and add water if it's needed. Add corn and lima beans, and cook until vegetables are tender, 5–10 minutes. While the vegetables are cooking, crumble the bacon. Spoon the vegetables into bowls, and sprinkle with bacon.

Minted Peas

MAKES 6 SERVINGS

4 cups green peas (about 3 lb. of
    fresh pods)

6 tbsp. butter, divided

1/2 medium onion, thinly sliced

1/4 cup chopped fresh mint

Sweet, tender, and tiny spring peas are delicious in this simple dish, but you can make it year-round with frozen peas, too. It makes use of the mint that grows abundantly in the South.

Melt 2 tbsp. butter in small skillet. Add onions and sauté until they are tender, about 5 minutes.

In a small saucepan, add just enough water to cover the bottom and keep the peas from scorching, about 1/4 cup. Add the peas and onion. Cover and cook over medium heat until peas are tender, 5–10 minutes, depending on size and freshness. If the butter is not at room temperature, melt it while the peas are cooking. When the peas are done, drain them, then add the butter and mint. Toss and serve immediately.

Creole Mixed Vegetables

Corn Pudding

2–2½ cups fresh corn (3–4 ears)

3 eggs, beaten with a fork

2 cups half and half

3 tbsp. butter

2 tbsp. sugar

1 tsp. salt

dash pepper

Corn pudding, a slightly sweet side dish, needs the milk of corn that is freshly scraped off the cob, so frozen or canned corn just won't do the job. This is a rich but simple dish, so you can dress it up with chopped peppers or fresh herbs.

Preheat oven to 350°F.

After you cut the corn off the cob, take a knife and rub the dull edge up and down the cob to force out whatever milk is left. Scrape this into a bowl with the corn.

Add the remaining ingredients and stir. Pour into an 8 × 8-inch baking pan, and bake at 350°F. Stir several times during the first half-hour of cooking, then leave it undisturbed for the last 15 minutes. Cook until pudding is slightly set, about 45–50 minutes in total.

Creamed Turnips and Peas

MAKES 6–8 SERVINGS

3 medium turnips (about 2 lb.)

3 cups young peas, preferably fresh

¼ cup chopped onion

¼ cup butter, divided

3 tbsp. flour

1½ cups milk

salt and pepper to taste

If you think you don't like turnips, you probably haven't tried them mixed with sweet young peas in a cream sauce. It is a substantial, comforting dish with a great taste.

Pare the turnips, cutting past the dark line that separates the rind from the white center. Slice turnips into fingers, like thick french fries. Drop the turnips into boiling salted water and cook, uncovered, until tender, about 15 minutes.

At the same time, cook the peas in boiling salted water until tender, 5–10 minutes.

While the vegetables are cooking, sauté the onion in 1 tbsp. butter until tender, about 5 minutes. Drain the turnips and peas. Mix turnips, peas, and onions in a large serving bowl. Cover to keep warm while you make the sauce.

Melt remaining 3 tbsp. butter in a small, heavy saucepan. Over low heat, whisk in flour until the mixture is smooth. Add milk, a little at a time, whisking constantly. Cook over low heat until the mixture thickens. Add salt and pepper to taste. Pour over vegetables and serve immediately.

Sweet Potato-Apple Soufflé

SERVES 4

2 cups cooked sweet potatoes, about 1 lb.

1 large tart apple, peeled and grated

2 tbsp. flour

4 tbsp. butter, melted

3 tbsp. molasses

1 tsp. grated lemon peel

1/2 tsp. salt

1/4 tsp. cinnamon

1/4 tsp. nutmeg

1/4 tsp. ground ginger

2 eggs, separated

1 egg white

1/4 tsp. cream of tartar

This soufflé rises only modestly, and doesn't have the dramatic crown of some soufflés. It is not temperamental, but if it doesn't puff up, don't tell anyone it was meant to be a soufflé. It has an excellent flavor and succeeds as a humble casserole. The molasses gives it a spicy, mildly sweet flavor.

Preheat oven to 400°F. Grease and flour a 5-cup soufflé dish, making sure you grease sides all the way to the top.

Purée sweet potatoes in blender or food processor. Grate apple and toss with flour (which will absorb any liquids that run out of apple as it cooks). Mix apple and sweet potato, then add all remaining ingredients except egg whites and cream of tartar.

In a separate bowl, beat 3 egg whites and cream of tartar until soft peaks form. Gently fold about 1/3 of the egg whites into the sweet potatoes, then fold in the rest. Stir the mixture as little as possible in order to keep the egg whites airy. Pour the mixture into the soufflé dish. Bake at 400°F until top is lightly browned, about 35 minutes.

Roast Corn

MAKES 6 SERVINGS

6 ears of corn, husks on

1/2 cup butter, softened to room
   temperature

2 tbsp. minced fresh chives

1 tsp. paprika

It's hard to improve on corn when it is fresh-picked, sweet, and tender. And when it's so easy to boil it, why bother? Roast corn is only slightly more work, and the result is different but delicious. This recipe uses butter that has been seasoned with fresh chives and paprika, but you can substitute other fresh herbs and spices to suit your taste — basil, oregano, cumin, cayenne, and chili powder all work well. Or brush the corn with garlic-flavored olive oil.

Mound a pyramid of coals in the center of the barbecue, and set alight.

Pull down the corn husks but don't remove them. Remove the silks and rinse the corn. Wipe the corn dry. Note: If your grocer has already removed all or part of the husks, you can use foil instead.

Put the softened butter in a small bowl with the chives and paprika. Mash the butter with a fork until the chives and paprika are well mixed into it. Spread a

scant amount of butter on each ear of corn. You don't want to use more than half the butter on this step. If you do, make more seasoned butter to serve on the side. Pull the husks back up so all the corn is covered. If there are no husks or if they have been trimmed to expose part of the corn, wrap each ear in foil.

When the barbecue flames have died and the coals are glowing and covered with ash, put the corn around the edges of the grill, not over the coals. Cover the barbecue. Cook the corn 20 minutes if it is young and tender, 25 minutes if the kernels are large. Turn several times during the cooking, so that all sides are exposed to the heat. When the corn is done, quickly remove the husks or foil and roll the ears around on the grill above the coals for just a minute or two, so that they begin to show spots of browning.

Serve the corn with the remaining seasoned butter on the side.

Fried Corn

MAKES 4 SERVINGS

3 cups corn (4–5 ears)

4 tbsp. butter

1/2 sweet red pepper, diced

1/2 cup chopped green onion

1/2 cup heavy cream

1 tsp. sugar

1/2 tsp. nutmeg

1/8 tsp. cayenne

optional: minced jalapeno
   chile, according to taste

When there's an abundance of sweet, summer corn and you're looking for a change from corn on the cob — as simple and delicious as that is — try fried corn cooked in cream. You can use frozen corn, but it's better with fresh corn.

Cut the corn from the cob, then scrape the cobs with the dull edge of a knife to

squeeze out any remaining milk.

Melt the butter in a skillet. Add the corn and corn milk, and cook over medium heat 5 minutes, stirring frequently. Add the red pepper and green onion and the jalapeno, if desired, and cook 2 minutes longer. Add remaining ingredients. Cook 3 minutes.

Roast Corn

Grilled Vidalia Onions

MAKES 4 SERVINGS

2 large Vidalia or other sweet
    onions
olive oil

Sweet onions — whether they are from Vidalia, Walla Walla, Maui, or any of the other areas that grow sweet onions — are far more versatile than the usual yellow onion. Sweet onions are so good that you can use them alone as a vegetable dish, instead of just as seasoning in another vegetable dish. One of the simplest ways to cook them is to grill them with a little olive oil. The oil can be plain or seasoned with garlic or herbs. Grilled Vidalia onions are an excellent accompaniment to grilled fish or fowl.

Peel onions and cut a thin slice off either end of each onion, so it can sit flat. Cut onions in half. Brush cut sides with plain or herbed olive oil. Place onion halves, cut side down, on grill over coals that are at the white-ash stage. Turn over after 4–5 minutes and cook for another 4–5 minutes, until outer layers are tender.

★ *ABOVE Richland Creek runs through the Ozark National Forest. The forest covers about 1.5 million acres of land in the mountains of northwestern Arkansas.*

Vidalia Onion Pie

MAKES 6 MAIN DISH OR 8 SIDE
DISH SERVINGS

9-inch deep-pie crust, pre-baked
3 medium Vidalia onions, peeled
    and thinly sliced (about 1 lb.)
2 tbsp. butter
1 cup grated Swiss cheese
3 eggs, beaten with a fork
2/3 cup sour cream
1/3 cup milk
1 tsp. salt
1/4 tsp. pepper

Sweet onions sautéed slowly until they are golden, Swiss cheese, and custard: this pie is delicious! Serve it as a main dish with a green salad and French bread, or as a side dish with grilled meat or fish. Use Vidalias or any sweet onion.

Melt the butter in a large skillet. Add the onions and sauté over low heat until they are golden brown, 25–30 minutes. Note: If your skillet isn't very large, you may have to use two skillets. Put the onions in the pie crust. Sprinkle grated Swiss cheese over the onions.

    Preheat the oven to 350°F.

    Make the custard by combining remaining ingredients. Pour custard over onions. Bake until custard is set and lightly browned around edges, about 45 minutes. Serve warm.

Green Beans and New Potatoes in Pesto

SERVES 4

1 lb. green beans, washed and trimmed

1 lb. tiny new potatoes, washed and cut in half

2 tbsp. pine nuts or chopped walnuts

1 clove garlic, peeled

1 cup loosely packed fresh basil leaves

⅔ cup Parmesan or Romano cheese, freshly grated if possible

⅓ cup olive oil

¼ tsp. salt

dash of black pepper

Although this dish takes advantage of the bounty of summer gardens, it can be made with potatoes and green beans that are available year-round, and pesto that is made in quantity during the summer, and frozen in small batches. It is a simple dish, and can be assembled in minutes if the pesto is made ahead of time.

Boil potatoes until tender, about 10 minutes. Boil green beans until tender, 3–4 minutes. While potatoes and beans are cooking, put remaining ingredients in food processor and process for about 10 seconds, until basil is well chopped but the mixture is not turned into a paste.

Drain potatoes and beans. Toss with pesto.

Green Bean Bundles

SERVES 4

1 lb. fresh green beans, washed and trimmed

8 strips of bacon

1/2 cup water

3 tbsp. brown sugar

1/2 tsp. cinnamon

1/4 tsp. cloves

1/2 tsp. dry mustard

1/4 tsp. salt

Bacon and brown sugar syrup are complementary flavors in this recipe, nicely setting off the taste of fresh green beans. The beans and bacon can be partially cooked and assembled in advance, cutting down on last-minute kitchen chores.

Preheat oven to 350°F. Lightly grease 8 × 8-inch baking pan or other wide, shallow casserole dish.

Cook green beans in boiling water for 2–4 minutes, until they are tender. (Cooking time will depend on whether beans are tough.) Drain, rinse with cold water, drain again, and set aside.

Partially cook bacon in skillet – long enough for some of the fat to cook out of the bacon, but not so long that it becomes crisp. The bacon must remain flexible. Remove bacon from skillet, and drain on paper towels.

Divide beans into eight bundles. Wrap each bundle with a strip of bacon and secure with a toothpick. Place bundles in baking pan.

Bring 1/2 cup water to a boil. Add sugar and spices, and bring barely to a boil. Pour syrup over beans.

Bake the beans, spooning syrup over the bundles once or twice during baking, until bacon is cooked, 10–15 minutes.

Greens and Dumplings

MAKES 4–6 SERVINGS

GREENS

2 lb. any combination of mixed greens

1 1/2–2 lb. smoked ham hocks

1 onion, peeled and quartered

2 dried red chiles

DUMPLINGS

3/4 cup cornmeal

1/2 cup flour

2 tsp. baking powder

1/2 tsp. salt

1/8 tsp cayenne

1 egg, lightly beaten with fork

1/3 cup milk

2 tbsp. melted butter

1/3 cup slivered ham (from ham hocks cooked with greens)

Greens are traditionally served with cornbread, so here we combined them into one dish. A mixture of greens is cooked with ham and onion, then topped with cornmeal dumplings. In the South, many greens grow wild, and some are available year-round. You can use any combination of turnip, dandelion, collard, mustard, kale, or other bitter greens. Rinse them well by immersing them in at least two baths of clean water. Otherwise, they're likely to be gritty. Cut off the thickest stems, then tear the leaves and tender stems into pieces.

Put ham and onion in stockpot. Add 3 quarts of water and boil for 1 hour to develop flavor. While the water is boiling, clean the greens. Add them to the water with the dried chiles. Simmer over medium heat until the greens are tender, about 1 hour (including the time while the dumplings are cooking).

About 30 minutes before greens are done, remove ham hocks. Cut off the meat and chop it finely. Set aside 1/3 cup for dumplings, and return the rest of the chopped ham to the greens.

To make the dumplings, combine the dry ingredients. In a small bowl, combine the egg, milk and melted butter, then pour into the dry ingredients. Mix well. Add the chopped ham and stir.

Pull off walnut-sized chunks of batter, shape into balls and flatten slightly. Carefully place the raw dumplings on top of the greens. Cover and cook about 20 minutes, until dumplings are cooked.

Green Bean Bundles

Baked Tomatoes

MAKES 4 LARGE OR
8 SMALL SERVINGS

4 large tomatoes, firm but ripe

salt

2 tbsp. olive oil

3 cloves garlic, minced

⅔ cup dried breadcrumbs

2 tbsp. chopped fresh basil,
*   or 2 tsp. dried*

2 tsp. chopped fresh oregano,
*   or ½ tsp. dried*

2 tbsp. finely minced green onion

⅓ cup Parmesan cheese

Baked tomatoes are too often regarded as a garnish rather than a serious vegetable. Maybe that's because we've been served too many soggy tomatoes with tasteless toppings. Here are some tips for making memorable baked tomatoes: Use tomatoes that are firm, not overripe. Time the cooking so you are ready to eat the tomatoes as soon as they come out of the oven. They don't keep well. Make your own crisp breadcrumbs by toasting good bread, and grinding it coarsely, rather than using bland, finely ground commercial breadcrumbs.

Preheat oven to 425°F. Lightly grease a shallow baking pan.

Core tomatoes and cut them in half. Lightly salt the cut sides, and turn the tomatoes cut side down on paper towels to drain while you prepare the topping.

Heat oil in small skillet. Add the garlic and sauté for 1–2 minutes, stirring and watching carefully so it doesn't scorch. If the oil is very hot, you may want to remove the pan from the burner. Add the breadcrumbs, return pan to the heat and cook 2 minutes, stirring almost constantly. Add the herbs and onion, continue cooking for about 30 seconds, and remove the pan from the heat. Stir in the Parmesan cheese.

Place tomatoes, cut side up, in a lightly oiled baking pan. Divide topping among tomatoes. Bake at 425°F until the tomatoes lose their firmness but are not mushy, 15–20 minutes. Serve immediately.

★ *ABOVE Paddlewheelers, popular along the Mississippi River in the middle of the 19th century, have returned to the river as tourist attractions.*

SIDE DISHES

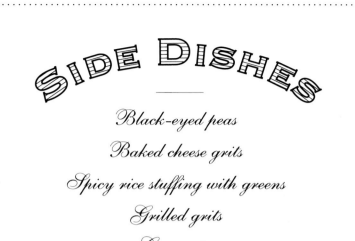

Black-eyed peas

Baked cheese grits

Spicy rice stuffing with greens

Grilled grits

Green rice

Fried apples and pears

Sausage stuffing

Fried potato patties

Fried sweet potatoes

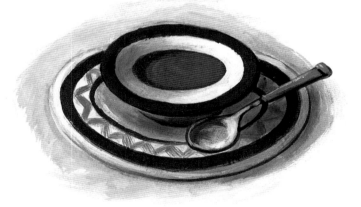

★ **OPPOSITE** *Spanish moss in one of the beautiful gardens in Louisiana.*

Black-eyed Peas

MAKES 6–8 SERVINGS

2 cups dried black-eyed peas

3–4 oz. salt pork

1 medium onion, cut into chunks

1 dried red chile

2 medium tomatoes, seeded and
    chopped

4 green onions, chopped

1/2 green pepper or mild chile
    (such as anaheim), chopped

2 tbsp. cider vinegar

2 tsp. sugar

salt and pepper

4 cups cooked rice

This rice and black-eyed peas dish is a variation on Hoppin' John, the dish that many Southerners insist must be eaten every January 1st for good luck in the New Year. A simple salsa-like topping adds flavor and color. You can spice it up even more by adding half a jalapeno pepper, finely chopped, to the topping.

Wash peas, and soak them overnight in 8 cups of water. Rinse. Place in large pan or medium stockpot with 6 cups water. Bring to a boil. Add salt pork, onion, and dried chile. Simmer until peas are soft and most of the water is absorbed, an hour or a little longer. You may add a little salt and pepper at the end, if you wish.

Make the topping by mixing together the tomatoes, green onions, green pepper, vinegar, and sugar. Add salt and pepper to taste.

Serve black-eyed peas over rice, and top with the tomato mixture.

Baked Cheese Grits

SERVES 6–8

4 cups milk

1 cup grits

½ tsp. paprika

pinch of salt

8 tbsp. (1 stick) butter, cut into
   pieces

2 eggs, lightly beaten

1 cup grated Cheddar cheese

This traditional casserole of grits and cheese can be eaten for breakfast or as a side dish with dinner. Any leftovers can be fried, grilled, or simply reheated. This recipe uses regular grits, and a long stovetop cooking time is necessary to achieve the proper mellow flavor. Otherwise, the casserole will have a sharp, raw taste. You can cut the cooking time if you use quick-cooking grits, but purists swear the flavor isn't as good.

Preheat oven to 350°F. Lightly butter a casserole with at least a 6-cup capacity.

Heat 3½ cups milk to just below the boiling point. Add grits, paprika, and salt. Stir constantly over medium heat until the grits absorb the milk and the mixture thickens, about 5 minutes. Continue cooking over low heat, stirring almost constantly, until grits lose their raw flavor, 20–25 minutes. Add butter and stir until it is melted and blended. Mix eggs with remaining ½ cup milk. Add egg mixture and cheese to grits, stirring until well blended. Pour grits into a casserole dish. Bake at 350°F until mixture sets and top is lightly browned, 45–55 minutes.

Spicy Rice Stuffing with Greens

MAKES ABOUT 5 CUPS OF STUFFING

2 cups cleaned and chopped
 mustard greens

2–4 tbsp. vegetable oil

1 cup chopped onion

¼ cup chopped celery

½ cup chopped green pepper

2 garlic cloves, minced

1 cup chicken stock

¼ tsp. black pepper

¼ tsp. salt

¼ tsp. cayenne

½ tsp. dry mustard

¼ tsp. ground cumin

⅓ cup slivered almonds, toasted
 (see note)

3 cups cooked rice

2 green onions, chopped

This rice dish was designed as a stuffing, but you can serve it as a side dish, too. The almonds add crunch, and the greens add a subtle flavor. This recipe calls for mustard greens, but you can substitute another type of greens if you prefer.

Wash the mustard greens at least twice. Run enough water into the sink to cover the greens. Swish the greens through the water, lift them out, and drain the water. Then rinse any sand from the sink, refill with fresh water and clean again, until all the grit has been washed out. Dry the greens with paper towels or in a salad spinner. Cut out and discard the coarse part of the stem. Chop the greens into 1-inch pieces. In a medium skillet, sauté the greens in 2 tbsp. oil until the greens are limp, 4–5 minutes. Remove the greens from the pan and set aside.

Add oil to the pan if needed, and sauté the onion, celery, green pepper, and garlic until they are tender, about 5 minutes. Add the chicken stock and spices. (If the rice was not cooked with salt, add another 1 tsp. salt.) Cook over medium heat until the liquids are slightly reduced. Add the greens, almonds, rice, and green onions. Stir well. Any excess stuffing can be cooked 20 minutes, covered, in a lightly oiled casserole dish.

Note: To toast almonds, spread in a single layer on baking sheet. Bake in 350°F oven until lightly browned, about 10 minutes. Be warned though – the almonds turn quickly from light brown to black.

Grilled Grits

MAKES 4–6 SERVINGS

1 cup grits
4½ cups water
1 tsp. salt
¼ cup butter
Olive oil
Parmesan cheese

Here's one way to use leftover grits. Thick slices of cold grits are brushed with oil and grilled, giving them a crusty outside and a creamy inside. But you may find you like grilled grits so much that you'll cook grits just so you can grill them. A tip: you won't lose slices of grits through the wide spaces in your barbecue grill if you use a rack specially made for cooking smaller items on top of the grill.

Put water, grits and salt in a heavy saucepan. Bring mixture to a boil and cook, stirring almost constantly, until the raw taste of the grits has mellowed, 30–40 minutes. Cut the butter into pieces and add to the grits, beating until the butter is melted and mixed in. Scrape the grits into a lightly buttered loaf pan. Chill.

Cut a loaf of grits into ¾-inch slices. Lightly brush all the edges with olive oil. If you have seasoned olive oil, or have time to let some garlic and rosemary sit in it ahead of time, that's even better.

Put the oiled slices on the barbecue grill when the flames have died to a glow and the coals are covered with white ash. Cook 4–5 minutes, until the underside is seared in the spots where it touches the grill and lightly browned elsewhere. Turn. Sprinkle the top with Parmesan cheese and cook another 4–5 minutes. Serve immediately.

Green Rice

MAKES 6–8 SERVINGS

3 cups water
1 tsp. salt
1 tsp. grated lemon peel
2 cloves garlic, peeled and minced
4 tbsp. butter, divided
1½ cups white rice
1½ cups chopped watercress
1 cup chopped onion
½ cup chopped green onion
¼ cup chopped parsley
½ tsp. black pepper
salt to taste

Watercress, onions, and parsley give color and flavor to rice in this dish. For extra flavor, cook the rice in chicken or vegetable broth.

Bring water, salt, lemon peel, garlic, and 2 tbsp. butter to a boil. Add the rice, stir well, cover, and reduce heat. Cook the rice at low heat until it is tender and the water is absorbed, 20–25 minutes.

While the rice is cooking, rinse the watercress thoroughly. Remove the leaves and chop. Melt remaining 2 tbsp. butter in a skillet. Sauté onions for 5 minutes, then add watercress and remaining ingredients and sauté 5 minutes longer. Stir into cooked rice.

Fried Apples and Pears

MAKES 4 SERVINGS

2 tart apples

2 pears

3 tbsp. butter

2 tbsp. brown sugar

¼ tsp. cinnamon

pinch of nutmeg

Wedges of apples, fried in butter with a little sugar sprinkled over them, are a popular side dish in the South, especially at breakfast. They're also good at lunch or dinner as an accompaniment to pork. This variation uses a mixture of tart apples and whatever pears are in season.

Peel and core the apples and pears, and cut them into thin wedges. Melt butter in a skillet. Add the apples and sauté over medium heat for 2 minutes. Add the pears. Mix the sugar, cinnamon and nutmeg, and sprinkle it over the fruit. Continue cooking until the apples and pears reach desired firmness, 10–15 minutes.

Sausage Stuffing

MAKES 6–8 SERVINGS

2 tbsp. butter

¾ cup chopped onion

¼ cup chopped celery

¼ cup chopped green pepper

2 small tart apples, peeled, cored, and chopped

½ lb. sausage meat

2 cups stale cornbread crumbs

2 cups stale white or wholewheat breadcrumbs

1½ tsp. fresh thyme, or ½ tsp. dried

1 tsp. fresh sage, or ¼ tsp. dried

2 tbsp. fresh parsley

½ tsp. salt

¼ tsp. pepper

⅛ tsp. cayenne

4–6 tbsp. milk or chicken broth

Cornbread stuffing made with sausage and apple goes well with a holiday turkey, a Sunday roast chicken, or as a side dish any day of the week. Directions here are for a side dish, or you may follow other directions for stuffed poultry. Start with the skillet cornbread recipe, or your favorite cornbread recipe.

Preheat oven to 350°F. Lightly butter a casserole dish (about 6-cup capacity).

Sauté onion, celery, and green pepper in 1 tbsp. butter for 5 minutes. Remove from pan with slotted spoon, and put in a large mixing bowl. Add butter to the skillet if necessary, and sauté the apples 5 minutes. Remove and add to the mixing bowl. Crumble the sausage meat into the skillet, and fry until lightly browned. Remove from pan with a slotted spoon and add to the mixing bowl. You may save the fat and use it to flavor and moisten the dressing instead of part of the milk or broth, if you wish.

Add the breadcrumbs and seasonings to the bowl and mix well. Add milk, broth, or fat to moisten. Stuffing should almost but not quite adhere in a solid mass. Put the stuffing in the casserole dish. Bake 30 minutes at 350°F.

Fried Potato Patties

MAKES 8 SERVINGS

2 lb. potatoes, peeled

6 strips of bacon

¼ cup butter

2 eggs, lightly beaten with a fork

1 tsp. salt

¼ tsp. paprika

¼ tsp. pepper

2 tbsp. chopped chives

1 cup grated cheddar cheese

1 egg

1 tbsp. milk

about 1¼ cups cracker crumbs

oil for frying

Mashed potatoes are seasoned with cheese and bacon, formed into patties and dipped in cracker crumbs, then fried until golden.

Boil the potatoes in salted water until they are tender, about 30 minutes, depending on the size of the potatoes. While the potatoes are cooking, fry the bacon until it's crisp, then drain on paper towels. Crumble the bacon.

When the potatoes are done, drain the water. Mash the potatoes with the butter, 2 eggs, salt, paprika, pepper, and chives. Mix in the cheese and crumbled bacon.

Form the potatoes into 8 patties. The patties will be soft, so handle them gently. Lightly beat the remaining egg with 1 tbsp. milk. Dip each patty in the egg mixture, then in the cracker crumbs, so it is coated on all sides.

Heat 1–2 tbsp. oil in a large skillet or 2 small skillets. Carefully add the potato patties. Cook over medium heat until golden brown on bottom, then turn and cook other side, about 7 minutes a side.

Fried Sweet Potatoes

MAKES 4 SERVINGS

2 large sweet potatoes

8 strips of bacon

2 tbsp. bacon fat, butter or olive oil

1 cup chopped onion

½ cup chopped green pepper

1 tsp. salt

¼ tsp. pepper

⅛ tsp. cayenne

Instead of hash browns, fry diced sweet potatoes with onions and bacon for a side dish that goes as well with eggs at breakfast as with pork chops at dinner. For a spicier dish, add a minced jalapeno chile.

Parboil sweet potatoes in boiling water for 15 minutes. Drain and peel potatoes, and cut them into slices ½-inch thick. Immerse the slices in a bowl of water to cool them.

Dice potatoes. While the potatoes are cooling, cook the bacon. When it is crisp, crumble it.

In 2 tbsp. bacon fat, butter or olive oil, sauté the onion and green pepper 5 minutes. Add the diced sweet potatoes and seasonings. Cook, stirring occasionally, until the potatoes are tender, 10–15 minutes. Add the bacon bits, and cook for another minute.

SEAFOOD

Pecan-smoked trout with horseradish sauce

Crab cakes

Baked catfish

Mint-grilled sea bass in tomato-mint salsa

Stuffed trout

Catfish with shrimp sauce

Spicy shark kabobs

Piquant shrimp

Bacon-grilled shrimp

Fish fillets in papillotte

Crab-stuffed zucchini

★ *OPPOSITE* *Shrimp fishing boats.*

Pecan-Smoked Trout with Horseradish Sauce

MAKES 4 SERVINGS

4 whole trout, cleaned and boned

3 quarts water

1 cup salt

2–3 cups pecan shells

*¹⁄₃ cup broken pecan pieces,
    optional*

horseradish sauce, recipe follows

Smoking trout at home on your covered barbecue is simpler than you might expect. And adding pecan shells instead of hickory or mesquite chips gives the trout a distinctly Southern character. Buy whole pecans and shell them yourself. Leave some whole nuts in the mix, and just crack their shells.

Place the trout, opened and skin side down, in a wide, shallow dish. Mix the salt and water, and pour over the fish. Let the fish sit in the brine, refrigerated, for no more than two hours or it will be too salty.

Soak the pecan shells in water for 30–40 minutes before you put them on the fire. Build a fire to one side in your covered barbecue, and let the coals burn down, until they are glowing and covered with white ash. Add 4–5 fresh coals. Drain the pecan shells and put them on the coals. Let them smoke for about 10 minutes. Oil the grill.

Remove the trout from the brine and rinse thoroughly.

Make sure any new flames have died down. Place the fish skin-side down on the barbecue grill, preferably not over the coals. If you wish, sprinkle the broken pecan pieces over the fish. Put the cover on the grill and let the fish smoke until their flesh flakes, 30–40 minutes.

The fish can be served hot or cold, with horseradish sauce on the side.

To make the horseradish sauce mix all ingredients and serve.

HORSERADISH SAUCE

¹⁄₂ cup sour cream

¹⁄₂–1 tsp. grated horseradish

1 tsp. dried dill

Crab Cakes

1 lb. crabmeat

2 eggs, lightly beaten with a fork

1 tbsp. fresh lemon juice

1/2 cup cracker crumbs

3 tbsp. mayonnaise

1/2 cup chopped green onion

1 tbsp. capers, drained

1 tsp. dry mustard

few drops Tabasco sauce

1/4 tsp. salt

dash of pepper

butter for frying

From Maryland to New Orleans, crab cakes are one of the most popular dishes in the South's coastal states. Crabmeat is mixed with seasonings, a small amount of crumbs, and eggs to bind the mixture, which is then shaped into cakes and fried. You can serve them as a main dish, as the large cakes in this recipe suggest, or shape them into smaller balls and serve them as hot hors d'oeuvres. Some cooks dip the uncooked crab cakes into egg and more crumbs before frying, but the crab flavor is more dominant without the additional coating of crumbs. Although fresh crab is recommended, frozen crab, and even canned crab in a pinch, also work well. Serve the crab cakes with a good tartar sauce, or a mayonnaise that has been spiced up with minced garlic and fresh tarragon or dill.

Pick through the crabmeat for bits of shell and cartilage. Mix by hand with all ingredients except the butter. Shape into 8 patties.

Melt butter in skillet. Fry the crab cakes over medium heat, turning once, until they are golden brown, about 4–5 minutes a side. Serve hot.

Baked Catfish

MAKES 4 SERVINGS

4 catfish fillets, about 6 oz. each

fresh lemon juice

olive oil

salt

pepper

paprika

Instead of frying catfish, bake them with a minimum of fat and top them with this crisp topping of highly seasoned crumbs.

Preheat oven to 350°F. Lightly oil a shallow baking pan.

Put catfish fillets in baking pan. Squeeze lemon juice over fillets, brush very lightly with olive oil, and sprinkle with salt, pepper, and paprika.

To make the topping, heat ⅓ cup olive oil in heavy skillet. Add the garlic and stir for 1 minute, taking care it doesn't scorch. If the oil is hot enough, you may be able to remove the pan from the burner, and the garlic will continue cooking in the hot oil. Reduce heat. Add the spices to the oil.

Cook, stirring constantly, just long enough to develop the flavor of the spices, about 1 minute. Again, you may be able to remove the pan from the burner, and the heat from the oil will be enough to cook the spices. The spices should stay a reddish-orange color. If the mixture browns, the spices are probably scorched and too bitter to use. Add the cornbread crumbs and cook, stirring almost constantly, 5 minutes.

Spoon the seasoned crumbs over the catfish fillets. Cover the baking pan and bake 10 minutes at 350°F. Remove the cover and bake 10–15 minutes longer, until the fish flakes easily.

TOPPING

⅓ cup olive oil

4 garlic cloves, pressed

¼ tsp. cayenne

¼ tsp. ground cloves

1 tsp. dry mustard

½ tsp. pepper

1 tsp. ground cumin

1 tsp. paprika

½ tsp. ground coriander

2 cups cornbread crumbs

Mint-Grilled Sea Bass with Tomato-Mint Salsa

MAKES 4 SERVINGS

4 sea bass steaks, about 6 oz. each

⅓ cup olive oil

2 tbsp. fresh lime juice

¼ cup chopped fresh mint

tomato-mint salsa (recipe follows)

This is an easy-to-fix dish that can be prepared in not much more time than it takes for the barbecue coals to burn down to glowing white ash. You can substitute any low-fat, firm-textured fish such as red snapper or halibut for the sea bass.

Mix the olive oil, lime juice and mint. Put the fish in a shallow glass or ceramic dish. Brush with the marinade, and pour any remaining marinade over the fish. Let the fish marinate for one hour.

While the fish are marinating, start the coals and prepare the salsa. Lightly oil the barbecue grill.

When the flames have died down and the coals are covered with white ash, place the fish on the grill. Cook until the fish flakes easily, about 10 minutes per inch of thickness, turning once during the cooking and brushing once or twice with leftover marinade.

For the salsa you don't absolutely have to grill the tomatoes and pepper, but you'll find that grilling gives them a nice smoky flavor.

When the coals are almost ready for the fish, put the tomato halves, cut side down, and the green pepper, skin side down, on the grill, just beyond the edge of the coals. Cook for 8 minutes. Put the charred pepper in a small plastic bag and close the bag while you chop the tomatoes. Mix with other ingredients. Remove pepper from bag. The steam will have softened the charred skin. Peel off the skin and chop the pepper, and add it to the salsa. Add salt and pepper to taste.

TOMATO-MINT SALSA

2 medium tomatoes, halved

1 half green pepper, cut into 2–3 relatively flat pieces

2 green onions, chopped

1–2 tbsp. chopped fresh mint

2 tsp. olive oil

1 tsp. cider vinegar

salt and pepper to taste

Stuffed Trout

MAKES 4 SERVINGS

1 tbsp. olive oil

1 tbsp. butter

½ cup chopped green onion

⅓ cup finely chopped celery

⅓ cup finely chopped green
    pepper

2 cloves garlic, minced

½ cup breadcrumbs

8 oz. cooked shrimp, any size, cut
    into bite-sized pieces

1 tbsp. fresh parsley

¼ tsp. salt

dash of pepper

dash of cayenne

4 trout, cleaned and boned, about
    ½-lb. each

olive oil

lemon juice

Trout are abundant in the South's lakes, as well as in much of the rest of the country, and should be readily available in most stores. However, you can substitute other small, whole fish such as rockfish.

Preheat oven to 350°F. Lightly grease a large baking sheet.

Heat the butter and olive oil in a medium skillet. Sauté the green onion, celery, green pepper and garlic until tender, about 5 minutes. Add breadcrumbs, shrimp, parsley, salt, pepper and cayenne, and cook about 2 minutes longer.

One by one, open each fish and place skin side down on a clean plate. Run a finger over the flesh to be sure all bones have been removed. Brush the inside of each fish lightly with olive oil, then squeeze a little lemon juice on each. Place one-fourth of the stuffing down the center of the fish. Fold the fish over, fasten with wooden toothpicks, and place on the baking sheet.

Bake at 350°F until the flesh of the trout flakes easily, about 20 minutes.

Catfish with Shrimp Sauce

MAKES 6 SERVINGS

6 catfish fillets, about 6 oz. each
(or 12 3-oz. fillets)
2 tbsp. olive oil
1 tbsp. fresh lemon juice
2 tsp. black pepper
2 tsp. paprika
sauce (recipe follows)

Catfish are a long-time staple of Southern cooking, but now that they are farmed commercially, fresh catfish are readily available in most cities. Here's a tasty alternative to the traditional fried catfish. Catfish fillets are briefly marinated, broiled, and topped with a chunky vegetable-and-shrimp sauce. Or cook the catfish in the sauce and serve over rice.

Put fish in a shallow glass or other non-reactive dish. Mix olive oil, lemon juice, pepper and paprika, and pour over catfish. Turn and spoon sauce over fish, so that all surfaces are coated. Let marinate about 30 minutes in refrigerator.

Put fish fillets on a lightly greased broiler pan. Spoon a little marinade over fillets. Broil, turning once, until fish lose their translucence and flake easily, about 10 minutes per inch of thickness.

To serve, spoon sauce over fish.

Making the sauce: if large prawns are used, cut each into several pieces.

In large skillet, sauté onion, celery, and green pepper in olive oil until tender, about 5 minutes. Mix the flour with a little of the fish stock or clam juice to make a smooth paste, then stir in the rest of the stock. Add it to the vegetables, and stir until well blended. Add Tabasco, Worcestershire, and lemon juice. Simmer about 2 minutes until sauce is thick and bubbly. Add shrimp, tomatoes, and green onion. Cook 2 minutes longer. Taste and add salt.

Alternative: Do not marinate or broil fish. Make the sauce. Cut the uncooked fish into strips 1–1½ inches wide. Add it to the sauce. Cover and cook over low heat, gently shaking the pan a few times. Don't stir as it may break up the fish. If the fish is not immersed in the sauce, gently turn the fish pieces once during cooking. Cook 6–8 minutes, or until the fish flakes easily. Serve over rice.

SAUCE

1 tbsp. olive oil
½ cup chopped onion
¼ cup chopped celery
¼ cup chopped green pepper
¾ cup fish stock or bottled clam
*   juice*
2 tbsp. flour
few drops Tabasco sauce
1 tbsp. Worcestershire sauce
1 tbsp. fresh lemon juice
6 oz. cooked shrimp, any size
1 cup fresh tomato, seeded and
*   chopped*
¼ cup chopped green onion
salt to taste

★ *ABOVE Dazzling sunset in Florida.*

Spicy Shark Kabobs

MAKES 4 SERVINGS

1½ lb. shark steak, cut into
  kabob-sized cubes

½ cup olive oil, divided

2 cloves garlic

2 tbsp. fresh lime juice

2 tbsp. ground cumin

2 tbsp. paprika

1 tsp. cayenne

2 tsp. freshly ground black pepper

1 small eggplant, cubed

1 zucchini, cut into half-inch
  slices

16 medium mushrooms

1 onion, cut into chunks

1 green or sweet red pepper, cut
  into chunks

A spice rub gives these chunks of fish and vegetables their piquant flavor, reminiscent of the popular blackened fish of New Orleans. The kabobs are grilled over a low to medium barbecue fire. Swordfish makes a delicious substitute for the shark.

If you are using wooden skewers, soak them in water for at least 30 minutes so they don't catch fire. Ignite barbecue coals about 30 minutes before you want to begin grilling.

Press two garlic cloves, and mix them with ¼ cup olive oil. (Or, if you have a microwave, crush two whole garlic cloves with flat side of knife. Put the oil and garlic cloves into a small microwave-safe bowl. Microwave oil on 50% power for 4–5 minutes, until garlic sizzles and is lightly browned.) Set the oil aside, letting the garlic steep.

Put cubes of shark in glass or ceramic bowl. Mix remaining ¼ cup olive oil with lime juice, and pour it over the shark. Toss the shark meat so that all the cubes are covered with the oil. Let the meat marinate about 20 minutes. Drain the fish. Combine cumin, paprika, cayenne and pepper. Then sprinkle about two-thirds of the spice mixture over the shark and toss so that all cubes are seasoned.

While fish is marinating, prepare vegetables. Place eggplant, zucchini, and mushrooms in a glass or ceramic bowl. Discard the garlic from the olive oil and pour the oil over the vegetables. Toss quickly to spread the oil evenly, since the vegetables soak up liquids like sponges. Sprinkle the remaining spice mix over the vegetables, and toss.

Thread the shark, seasoned vegetables, onion and pepper onto skewers. Do not press the pieces too tightly together, as they will not cook evenly. Lightly oil the barbecue grill. When coals are white and no longer flaming, place the skewers on the grill over the coals. Turn once or twice, until fish is flaky and loses its translucency — about 10 minutes total for every inch of the fish's thickness.

Piquant Shrimp

MAKES 4–6 SERVINGS

2 lb. medium or large shrimp,
    peeled and deveined

1 cup unsalted butter

½ cup olive oil

3 green onions, chopped

6 cloves garlic, minced or pressed

1 tbsp. chopped fresh basil,
    or 1 tsp. dried

1½ tsp. fresh oregano,
    or ½ tsp. dried

1 tsp. dried red pepper flakes

1 tsp. paprika

1 tsp. salt

1 tbsp. fresh lemon juice

This Cajun-inspired dish is simple to make, and most of the work can be done ahead of time. The shrimp is pleasantly spicy, but if you prefer your food mouth-searing hot, just increase the amount of red pepper flakes. Serve the shrimp with a good, dense bread like French or sourdough to sop up the rich butter sauce.

Preheat oven to 450°F.

To make the sauce, melt butter, then mix with all ingredients except shrimp. The sauce may be made a day in advance and refrigerated. (If you make the sauce in advance, you don't need to melt the butter or mix ingredients well. When you are ready to cook the shrimp, melt the whole mixture and blend well.)

Spread the shrimp in a 9 × 13-inch baking pan or other wide, shallow baking dish. Pour the sauce over the shrimp. Turn the shrimp so the sauce coats them all. Bake at 450°F until all shrimp are cooked, 5–10 minutes. They will curl tightly, lose their translucence, and turn white. You may need to turn the shrimp once or twice during cooking to be sure they cook evenly.

Bacon-Grilled Shrimp

MAKES 4 SERVINGS

1 lb. large shrimp, peeled and
   deveined

½ cup olive oil

2 tbsp. white wine vinegar

1 tbsp. fresh lemon juice

1 tbsp. Dijon-style mustard

3 cloves garlic, pressed

about 6 drops Tabasco sauce

sprigs of fresh rosemary

about 12 strips of bacon
   (½ strip per shrimp)

Large shrimp are soaked in a garlicky marinade, wrapped in rosemary and bacon, and finally grilled on skewers over hot coals. The bacon adds a wonderful flavor to the shrimp, but it also causes the coals to flare up, so the shrimp has to be watched closely and moved around as it cooks. Fortunately it doesn't take long to cook, and is delicious.

Make the marinade by mixing the olive oil, vinegar, lemon juice, mustard, garlic, and Tabasco. Put the shrimp in a shallow glass or other non-reactive bowl. Pour the marinade over the shrimp and stir so each piece is well coated. Refrigerate 1–2 hours, turning the shrimp several times.

If you are using wooden skewers, soak them in water for at least 30 minutes so they do not burn easily.

Cut the bacon strips in half. Place a small sprig of rosemary and a shrimp on each. Wrap the bacon around the shrimp and rosemary, and press the skewer through the shrimp and bacon. Don't crowd the shrimp together, but also don't leave large sections of wooden skewer exposed, as it may burn.

Grease the grill. When the coals are glowing and covered with ash, place the skewers of shrimp over the coals. As the bacon cooks, it will drip fat onto the coals and probably cause flames to spurt up. Move the skewers around as needed to keep them from catching fire, and turn the shrimp several times so all sides are exposed to the coals. The bacon will keep the shrimp juicy. They are done when the shrimp have lost their translucency and are white-pink all the way through, 5–10 minutes.

Fish Fillets en Papillote

MAKES 4 SERVINGS

4 fillets, about 6 oz. each

3 tbsp. butter, plus butter for
    parchment

2 cups coarsely chopped
    mushrooms

1/2 cup chopped green onion

1 tbsp. flour

2 tbsp. cream

1/4 tsp. salt

dash pepper

4 oz. crabmeat, preferably fresh

BUTTER SAUCE

1 tbsp. finely chopped green
    onion, white part only

2 tbsp. dry white wine or
    champagne

2 tbsp. white wine vinegar

6 tbsp. unsalted butter, cut into
    pieces

2 tbsp. heavy cream

1 tsp. chopped fresh tarragon, or
    1/2 tsp. dried

1/4 tsp. salt

dash white pepper

In the South, this dish is traditionally made with pompano, a delicate, gourmet fish. Pompano is expensive and fragile, so it is not readily available far from the warm waters of the Gulf. Substitute turbot, flounder, red snapper, or other lean and delicately flavored fillets. Bake the fillets in individual envelopes of parchment, available at most gourmet and kitchen stores. Foil works as well, but it is not as elegant at the table. You may serve butter sauce on the side, but the fish is good without it, too.

Pick over the crabmeat to make sure there are no bits of shell or cartilage. Lightly oil a large, shallow baking pan. Preheat the oven to 400°F.

Cut parchment into four hearts, each about 12 × 15 inches, but at least 3 inches longer than fillets. Lightly butter one side of the paper. Fold the hearts in half, with the buttered side on the inside. Place one fillet on the right side of each heart.

Make the topping. In butter in a medium skillet, sauté the mushrooms and green onions 10 minutes. Sprinkle flour over the mushrooms, stir, and cook 1 minute. Add cream, salt and pepper, stir, and cook 1 minute longer. Remove from heat. Gently stir in crabmeat.

Spoon the topping over the four fillets. Fold the left side of each heart over the top. Fold and crimp the edges of the paper so they form enough of a seal to trap the steam from the fish. Place the packets in the baking pan. Bake at 400°F until the fish flakes easily, about 15 minutes.

While the fish is baking, make the sauce.

Combine the onion, wine or champagne, and wine vinegar in a small saucepan. Bring to a boil and cook, stirring frequently and watching closely, until liquid reduces to 1 tbsp. Strain the liquid to remove the onion, and return the liquid to the pan. Whisk in the butter, one piece at a time. Then add cream, tarragon, salt and pepper, and whisk until smooth.

Crab-Stuffed Zucchini

**MAKES 4–8 MAIN COURSE
SERVINGS, DEPENDING ON
THE SIZE OF THE ZUCCHINI,
OR 8 FIRST COURSE SERVINGS**

4 fat zucchini

3 tbsp. vegetable oil

2/3 cup chopped onion

2/3 cup chopped celery

1/3 cup chopped green pepper

2 cloves garlic, minced

2/3 cup dried breadcrumbs

1 tsp. dried basil

1/2 tsp. dried thyme

1 tsp. salt

1/4 tsp. black pepper

1/4 tsp. cayenne

2–3 tbsp. milk or clam juice

3/4 lb. fresh crabmeat

Parmesan cheese

Fresh crabmeat is mixed with sautéed vegetables, herbs and breadcrumbs, then stuffed into hollowed-out zucchini halves. In Louisiana, the dish is called pirogues, after the dugout canoes used in the bayous, which they resemble. You can also try this filling in mirliton – also known as chayote – another squash popular in some parts of the South. Depending on the size of the zucchini, one boat can be a main course.

Preheat oven to 350°F. Lightly grease a large, shallow baking dish.

Cut the zucchini in half lengthwise. Scoop out the pulp, leaving a quarter-inch shell. Chop the pulp. Sauté it in the vegetable oil with the onion, celery, green pepper, and garlic until the vegetables are tender and excess moisture has evaporated, 10–12 minutes. Remove vegetables from the heat.

In a large bowl, mix breadcrumbs, herbs and spices, and cooked vegetables. Add enough milk or clam juice so that the mixture is moist, but not mushy.

With your fingers, pick through the crabmeat to remove any bits of bone or cartilage. Gently mix it into the stuffing. Mound the stuffing into the zucchini shells. Sprinkle with Parmesan cheese. Place the zucchini in the baking pan. Bake at 350°F until the zucchini is tender, about 20 minutes. Serve immediately.

MEAT & POULTRY

Barbecue including:

Spice rub

Basting sauce

Barbecue Sauce No. 1

Barbecue Sauce No. 2

Barbecued spare ribs

Barbecued pork shoulder

Ham

Chicken creole

Sausage and ham pie

Buttermilk chicken

Ham frittata

Citrus-fried chicken

Old-fashioned chicken and homemade noodles

Stuffed chicken thighs

Chicken pot pie with cornmeal crust

Roast pork with rhubarb sauce

Pork chops in mustard gravy

Chicken and shrimp pilau

Rabbit in mushroom-wine sauce

★ *OPPOSITE Caddo Lake, northwest of Shreveport on the Texas-Louisiana state line, was formed by the damming of the Red River by the Great Raft.*

BARBECUE

*L et's talk about **real** barbecuing. Not cooking directly over smouldering charcoal – that's grilling. Southern barbecuing is long, slow cooking in the smoke from the coals. It's not smoke-curing either. Smoking – which involves brining the meat first – occurs at about 100°F. Barbecuing takes place at temperatures between 180°F–220°F, under a covered grill, with the coals off to the side. This type of barbecuing is not for tender steaks and quick burgers, but for tough, fatty cuts of meat like pork shoulder and beef brisket, which are tenderized by slow cooking.*

From Texas to North Carolina to Tennessee and in between, the South boasts various regional styles of barbecuing. In Texas, barbecue means beef brisket with a ketchup-based sauce. In North Carolina, it's pork shoulder in a light vinegar-based sauce. In Tennessee, it's ribs crusted with a dry spice mixture.

Two kinds of sauces are used in barbecuing. The basting sauce, applied to the meat at regular intervals during cooking, is a simple, usually vinegar-based sauce whose purpose is to keep the meat from drying out during barbecuing. The finishing sauce, whether it is based on vinegar or ketchup, is served on the side or applied only during the last few minutes of cooking. This is particularly important if the sauce contains sugar, since the sugar will burn if it's applied early in the cooking process and so turn the sauce bitter. Most commercial barbecue sauce is finishing sauce, and it nearly always contains sugar.

Fuel is important, too. Because the smoke does the cooking over a long period, the fuel is a more dominant element in the flavor of the finished meat. For that reason, barbecue purists use hardwoods or briquettes made of hardwood rather than ordinary charcoal. Mesquite, oak, and hickory are most common. Some cooks top the embers with grapevines, rosemary branches, or other exotic woods to add extra flavor.

To build a barbecue fire, stack the coals in a pyramid at one side of the barbecue pit or kettle. The meat will cook at the other side of the

barbecue, not over the coals. Let the flames die down to glowing embers – usually about 40 minutes – before you put the meat on. If you want to add wood chips, grapevines or other flavor-enhancing woods to the fire, soak them in water first for about 30 minutes, then put them on the coals about 10 minutes before you're ready to put the meat on. You'll need to check the fire every half hour or so, and add coals or wood to replenish the burned-out ones. An inexpensive oven thermometer is handy for checking whether the fire is too hot.

Most meats need to be basted frequently during the cooking process in order to stay moist. The complication is that every time you lift the cover off the barbecue, the temperature drops, and it takes time to build up heat again. If you're cooking on a small barbecue, this can be beneficial because the temperature tends to run hot. On larger barbecue set-ups, try to make the basting coincide with the fire-checking times, although some meats, such as ribs, may need more frequent basting. Cooking times will vary according to the size of your fire, the distance between the coals and the meat, how often you remove the cover, and of course the cut of meat. Baby back ribs may be done in little more than an hour, while a big beef brisket may take 10 hours or longer. A meat thermometer – and a certain amount of flexibility in the dining hour – will come in handy.

Following are a recipe for dry spice rub, a basting sauce, and two styles of finishing sauces, as well as techniques for cooking ribs and pork shoulder.

Spice Rub

2 tbsp. salt
2 tbsp. sugar
2 tbsp. brown sugar
2 tbsp. ground cumin
2 tbsp. chili powder
2 tbsp. black pepper
2 tbsp. paprika
1 tbsp. cayenne

This mix is just a starting point. Vary the recipe to suit your own taste. Increase the cayenne if you like your food spicy-hot, omit the cumin if you don't like it, add other spices like ginger or turmeric for a more exotic flavor.

Combine all ingredients. Rub into surface of meat before cooking. Save any excess mix in a covered container.

Makes 1 cup rub, plenty for 2–3 pork shoulders, several whole chickens, or several racks of spareribs. It's enough for a small beef brisket, but a 10-lb. brisket will require two cups.

Basting Sauce

2 cups white vinegar
⅔ cup stale coffee
½ cup vegetable oil
1 tsp. cayenne
1 tsp. black pepper
1 tsp. dry mustard

You can substitute ingredients freely in basting sauce, as long as it's wet. Some people use warm beer, leftover wine, or orange juice instead of stale coffee. Add and subtract spices to suit your taste.

Makes 3 cups of basting sauce, enough for 2 pork shoulders, several chickens, or several racks of ribs. You may need to make a double batch for a big beef brisket, depending on how generously you apply the sauce and how long you cook the meat. But since the sauce is easy to make, you can quickly slap more together if it looks like you'll run out early.

★ *RIGHT Boasting about one's barbecue skills and secret sauces is a favorite sport in the South, which features many barbecue festivals and competitions, like this one in Owensboro in northwestern Kentucky.*

★ 105 ★

Barbecue Sauce No. 1

1 tbsp. vegetable oil
1/4 cup chopped onion
2 cloves garlic, minced
1 cup bottled chili sauce
6 oz. tomato paste
1/3 cup white vinegar
2 tbsp. Dijon-style mustard
1 tbsp. Worcestershire sauce
1 tsp. cream-style horseradish
1 tsp. lemon juice
1 tsp. celery seed
2 tbsp. brown sugar
1 tsp. freshly ground black pepper
1 tsp. chili powder
1/2 tsp. ground ginger
1/4 tsp. salt

If you were a real purist, you'd begin with fresh tomatoes and cook your sauce for hours. This recipe is a compromise between a from-scratch sauce, and doctored-up store-bought sauce. It produces a tangy, sweet-sour sauce that goes well with most meats.

In a heavy, medium-size saucepan, sauté the onion and garlic in the oil until the onion is tender, about 5 minutes. Add the remaining ingredients, and mix well. Bring to a boil, reduce heat, and cook over low heat for 10 minutes.

Brush sauce over meat just before removing it from the barbecue, or serve meat dry with sauce on the side.

Makes a little more than 2 cups sauce.

Barbecue Sauce No. 2

This peppery vinegar sauce is traditionally served with pork shoulder, but it's good on ribs, too.

Put the oil, garlic, and ginger in a small, microwave-safe bowl. Microwave at 50% power about 4 minutes, until garlic is lightly browned. If you don't have a microwave, put the garlic and ginger in the oil the night before you plan to use it, and let it sit in the refrigerator. When ready to use, press the garlic and ginger to squeeze out juices, then discard garlic and ginger.

Combine the flavored oil with remaining ingredients in a small saucepan. Bring to a boil, let cook for 2–3 minutes. Remove from heat. Serve hot or cold.

MAKES ABOUT 2 CUPS SAUCE
1/4 cup olive oil
3 cloves garlic, peeled and
  crushed
several nickel-sized slices of fresh
  ginger
1 1/2 cups cider vinegar
2 tsp. sugar
2 tsp. red pepper flakes
1/4 cup Dijon-style mustard
1 tsp. black pepper

★ *ABOVE* With their bright pink color, flamingos are a
popular sight for Florida tourists.

★ *OPPOSITE*
above: Spice Rub;
left: Barbecue Sauce No 1;
right: Basting Sauce

Barbecued Spareribs

MAKES 2 SERVINGS

1 large rack of spareribs, about 3 lb.

1 cup basting sauce

barbecue (finishing) sauce

Because of their thickness and their high fat content, spareribs — as distinguished from beef ribs, baby back ribs, or country-style pork ribs — are perfect for barbecuing. Their only drawback is their size. If you're cooking on a basic barbecue, you probably won't have room for more than one large rack of ribs, unless you have a rack that cooks racks of ribs upright. This recipe also works for baby back ribs, but because they're smaller and less fatty, they require more frequent basting and less cooking time.

When the flames have died and the coals are glowing embers, baste the ribs with some of the basting sauce. If the coals are very low, add some fresh coals. Place the ribs on a greased grill so they are not directly over the coals and so meatiest part is away from coals. Cover the barbecue, leaving the vent open. Baste the ribs about every 20 minutes, and add coals to the embers as needed. Ribs are done when meat in the thickest part is pinkish-white, about 1½–2 hours for spareribs, about 1 hour for baby back ribs.

Add finishing sauce just before you remove meat from the grill, or serve meat dry with sauce on the side.

Barbecued Pork Shoulder

MAKES ABOUT 12 SERVINGS

2 boneless pork shoulders or butts, about 4 lb. each

1 cup dry rub

3 cups basting sauce

2 cups Barbecue Sauce No. 2

Chopped pork sandwiches are the definition of barbecue in the Carolinas. The meat is cooked slowly to an internal temperature of 170°F. The shoulder is then chopped or shredded, with the fatty tissue separated out. The meat is mixed with a vinegary sauce, and served on white bread or hamburger buns.

About 2 hours before you put the meat on the barbecue, rub it all over with the dry rub. Let the meat sit out so it reaches room temperature. Just before cooking time, give the meat a touch-up application with the remaining dry rub.

Put the meat on the grill, fat side up, at the opposite side of the barbecue from the coals. Baste lightly with the basting sauce.

Don't worry about washing off the spice rub — enough will stay on to give it a crusty coating. Cover the grill, but vent it slightly.

Check and baste the meat every 30–40 minutes. Add coals to the fire as needed. If you're using a small barbecue, you may need to set the cover askew sometimes to bring the temperature down. The meat should take 4–6 hours to cook. The best and safest way to tell when the meat is done is with a meat thermometer. Pork should reach 170°F in its thickest part.

When the meat is cooked, shred or chop it. Discard the fatty tissue but save the crusty exterior — that's the best part. Mix with Barbecue Sauce No. 2, and serve with white bread or hamburger buns.

Ham

whole smoked country ham
1 cup cider vinegar
1 cup brown sugar
2 tsp. ground cloves
2 tbsp. dry mustard
¼ cup cornmeal
¼ cup cider vinegar, sherry,
    bourbon, or pineapple juice

The Southern country-style ham—lean, salty, and smoky—is a celebration of the old methods of preserving meat. In the days before refrigeration, the hind leg of the pig was cured with salt, smoked, and aged perhaps as long as two years. That long and complicated process is no longer necessary in order to preserve meat. But the result is so deliciously different from today's flabby hams that there is still a demand for old-fashioned country hams.

Country-style hams are rubbed with salt and spices, then left to cure for about a month. They are then smoked, with hickory being the favored fuel. The hams are aged from six months to two years. During the process, they absorb great quantities of salt and lose much of their moisture. Consequently, preparation of a true country-style ham takes two to three days, during which time excess salt is soaked out, and moisture is restored.

To prepare a whole smoked country ham, begin by scrubbing off the exterior mold with a stiff brush under running water. Place the ham in a large pot and cover it with water. Let it soak for 24 hours. Discard the water, and scrub the ham again. Put the ham in a large roasting pan with 1 cup of cider vinegar, and cover it with water. Roast it in the oven at 325°F for about 4 hours, turning once. Or cook it on the stovetop at a gentle simmer, covered, for about 4 hours, adding boiling water as needed to keep the ham covered. The ham should cook 15–18 minutes per pound.

Let the ham cool in the cooking water. This helps restore moisture. It will take several hours to reach room temperature.

You may let it sit out overnight while cooling.

When you are ready to cook the ham, preheat the oven to 400°F. Drain the ham and cut off the rind. Trim the fat, leaving only a ¼-inch layer.

Make a paste by mixing the brown sugar, cloves, dry mustard, cornmeal, and liquid of your choice.

Cover the ham with the paste. Bake for 30 minutes, then remove from oven and let it sit for 30 minutes to an hour.

Country ham is traditionally served sliced paper-thin. Serve it on Sweet Potato Biscuits (page 61) or beaten biscuits. Or eat it with rhubarb sauce (page 119, Roast Pork with Rhubarb Sauce).

A 15-lb. ham should serve 25–30 people.

★ *BELOW Horses graze on the pasturelands of Aiken, South Carolina, a short distance from the Savannah River.*

Chicken Creole

MAKES 6 SERVINGS

5 chicken half-breasts, boned and
   skinned
1 tbsp. flour
1 tsp. salt
1/4 tsp. dried thyme
1/2 tsp. dried oregano
1/2 tsp. dried basil
1/2 tsp. paprika
1/8 tsp. cayenne
1/8 tsp. black pepper
1/8 tsp. white pepper
4 tbsp. vegetable oil, divided
1 cup chopped onion
1 cup chopped green pepper
1 cup chopped celery
2 garlic cloves, minced
3 cups chicken stock
2 1/2 cups fresh tomatoes, seeded
   and chopped
8-oz. can tomato sauce
1 tsp. sugar
few drops Tabasco sauce
salt to taste
1/4 cup chopped parsley
3/4 cup chopped green onion
4 cups cooked rice

This Louisiana Creole dish is based on a rich, spicy tomato sauce that is cooked long and slow, then served over rice. The seasoning comes from the chicken, which is cubed, tossed with a spice mixture and sautéed before it is added to the pot. It's also good made with shrimp. This version shortcuts the traditional recipe, where chicken parts are simmered first to make homemade stock, but make your own stock if you have time.

Cut the chicken into bite-size cubes. Mix the flour and spices in a small bowl. Sprinkle the spices over the chicken, and toss the chicken so the cubes are evenly covered with spice. Heat 2 tbsp. oil in a skillet. Sauté the chicken until it is lightly browned and cooked through, about 10 minutes. Remove the chicken with a slotted spoon, and set aside.

Add the additional oil to the skillet, if necessary. Sauté the onion, pepper, celery, and garlic for 5 minutes.

In a large saucepan, bring the chicken stock to a boil. Add the chicken, sautéed vegetables, tomatoes, tomato sauce, and sugar. Simmer, covered, for 45 minutes, stirring occasionally. Add Tabasco and salt to taste. Just before serving, stir in the parsley and green onion. Spoon the Creole sauce over rice in bowls and serve.

Sausage and Ham Pie

MAKES 4–6 SERVINGS

FILLING

12 oz. bulk sausage

1 medium onion, chopped

1/2 cup chopped green pepper

1 cup diced ham

1 cup corn

2 medium tomatoes, seeded and
chopped

1 1/2 cups beef stock

1 tsp. chopped fresh sage, or 1/4
tsp. dried

1 tsp. chili powder

1/2 tsp. salt

1/4 tsp. pepper

This savory pie, cousin to the tamale pie, is a tasty way of using leftover ham. The casserole is topped with a cornmeal batter that sinks into the filling, then rises to become a crust. If there's a lot of liquid in your filling, the batter will absorb it and form a very high, but moist topping. The recipe suggests the addition of sage and chili powder, but you should adjust seasonings depending on the type of sausage you buy. If you use a sage-flavored sausage, the casserole won't need sage. If you buy a very hot and spicy sausage, you might want to omit the chili powder.

Crumble the sausage meat in a skillet, and sauté until it is browned. Remove sausage with a slotted spoon. Pour off all but 1 tbsp. fat, or add a little vegetable oil if necessary, to sauté onion and green pepper. Cook until vegetables are tender,

about 5 minutes. Put the sausage, cooked vegetables, and remaining filling ingredients in a large saucepan. Bring mixture to a boil and cook, uncovered, about 15 minutes to reduce some of the liquids. Pour the filling into a lightly greased 2-quart casserole dish.

To make the topping, preheat oven to 425°F.

Combine the dry ingredients. Cut in the shortening, then add the egg and mix well. Add enough milk so that the batter is pretty wet, but still adheres in a solid mass. Scoop out spoonfuls of batter, flatten them, and lay them on top of the filling. Some will sink. Don't attempt to form a solid crust, just try to distribute the batter fairly evenly.

Bake the casserole at 425°F until the cornmeal rises and forms a golden brown crust, about 25 minutes.

TOPPING

1 cup cornmeal

1/4 cup flour

1 tsp. sugar

1/2 tsp. salt

2 tsp. baking powder

2 tbsp. shortening

1 egg, lightly beaten

about 1/2 cup milk

Buttermilk Chicken

MAKES 4 SERVINGS

1 frying chicken, 3–3 1/2 lb., cut
up

3 cups buttermilk

1/2 cup dried breadcrumbs

1/4 cup cornmeal

1/3 cup Parmesan cheese

1/2 tsp. dried oregano

1 tsp. paprika

1/4 tsp. garlic powder

1/2 tsp. salt

1/4 tsp. pepper

Chicken is marinated in buttermilk, which gives it a subtle tang reminiscent of sour cream. It is then coated in a tasty mixture of crumbs, Parmesan cheese and spices, and baked. It's an easy and delicious alternative to fried chicken.

Trim fat and any excess skin off chicken pieces. Put the pieces in a glass, ceramic or plastic bowl, and pour the buttermilk over them. Let the chicken soak in the buttermilk all day or overnight.

Preheat oven to 400°F. Lightly grease a 9 × 13-inch baking pan.

Mix the remaining ingredients. Remove chicken from the buttermilk, and let it drain briefly. Dip each piece in the crumb mixture, and pat crumbs on any bare spots. Place the chicken in a baking dish, making sure not to crowd the pieces. Bake until the chicken is golden brown, and the juices run clear instead of pink, 40–50 minutes.

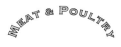

Ham Frittata

**MAKES 6 MAIN DISH
SERVINGS, OR
10–12 APPETIZER SERVINGS**

1 medium potato

2–4 tbsp. vegetable oil

1 large onion, thinly sliced

1 cup diced ham

1 cup grated Swiss cheese

salt and pepper to taste

6 eggs

A frittata is like an omelet, only easier because it's baked. It can be filled with all sorts of ingredients – diced chicken, crumbled bacon, small shrimp, cheeses, cooked vegetables, fresh herbs, salsa, or anything else you'd put in an omelet. A frittata is an Italian dish, and is sometimes served cold, in small wedges, as part of an antipasto platter, as well as for breakfast, lunch, or dinner.

Lightly oil a 9-inch or 10-inch baking dish, such as a deep-dish pie pan or a quiche dish.

Boil the potato in salted water until it is tender, about 30 minutes. While the potato is cooking, sauté the onion slices in 2 tbsp. olive oil over low heat until they are golden, 25–30 minutes. Remove the onions with a slotted spoon, and spread them evenly over the bottom of the baking dish.

Peel and dice the cooked potato. Add more oil to the skillet if necessary, and fry the potato over medium-low heat, turning occasionally, for 15 minutes.

Add the potato and the ham to the baking dish. Sprinkle with salt and pepper. Spread the grated cheese over the mixture. Put the eggs in a medium bowl and beat them briefly. Pour the eggs over the cheese.

Bake the frittata in a preheated 400°F oven until the eggs have puffed up, the center is set, and there is a little browning around the outside, 20–25 minutes. Cut into wedges and serve hot or cold.

Citrus-Fried Chicken

SERVES 4

1 frying chicken, cut up
¼ cup fresh lime juice
¼ cup fresh lemon juice
¼ cup fresh orange juice
¼ cup olive oil
*4 garlic cloves, peeled and
    crushed*
few drops Tabasco sauce
1 cup flour
1 tsp. salt
½ tsp. black pepper
vegetable oil or lard

From Florida, with its Caribbean influences, comes the inspiration for this tangy, crispy fried chicken. It is marinated in a mix of lemon, lime and orange juices, spiced with garlic and Tabasco sauce. For the best flavor, use fresh-squeezed juices.

Make the marinade by mixing fruit juices, olive oil, garlic, and Tabasco. Trim any excess fat off the chicken and remove skin, if desired. Put the chicken pieces in a glass or other non-reactive dish. Pour the marinade over the chicken, making sure that each piece is coated. Marinate in refrigerator at least 3 hours, or overnight.

Mix flour, salt, and pepper in a bowl or a paper bag. Dip or shake each chicken piece in the flour mixture so that there is a thin coating of flour over the entire piece. Knock off any excess.

Heat oil or lard in a heavy skillet. The oil should be about ½–1 inch deep, and very hot. Carefully place chicken in the hot oil. The pieces should not be crowded. You probably will need to fry the chicken in two batches (keep the first batch warm in the oven while the second is cooking), or use two skillets. Fry over medium to medium-high heat, depending on your stove and the heaviness of the skillet. Watch carefully so that the chicken does not burn. It is done when the meat juices run clear, about 20–25 minutes.

Old-Fashioned Chicken and Homemade Noodles

MAKES 4 SERVINGS

1 chicken, cut in half or into
    serving pieces
several extra backs and necks
2 carrots, cut in several pieces
2 stalks celery, leaves included,
    cut in several pieces
1 onion, quartered
several sprigs of parsley
2 bay leaves
1 tsp. peppercorns
½ lb. (about 3 cups) sliced
    mushrooms
2 tbsp. butter
salt and pepper to taste
Noodles (recipe follows)

This is a variation on a dish my grandmother, Letty Belden, makes for Sunday dinner. It is not difficult and you don't need a pasta machine, but it is time-consuming. If possible, cook the chicken and stock the night before. Not only will it save time the next day, but it will be easier to remove the fat from the stock after it has cooled in the refrigerator overnight. The noodles should be made early in the day because they need several hours of drying time.

Put chicken, extra backs and necks, carrots, celery, onion, parsley, bay leaves, and peppercorns in a stockpot. Add enough cold water to cover the chicken, plus about 2 inches more. Bring water to a boil. Skim off scum as it rises to the top. Let the stock simmer until the meat is falling off the bone, about 90 minutes. Remove the chicken (but not the necks and backs) from the pot, and return the stock to the heat. Let the chicken cool slightly. Pull the meat from the bones. Add the skin and bones back to the stock. Refrigerate the the meat, and let the stock cook about another hour. You will need 6–8 cups of chicken stock, measured after the fat has been removed.

Strain the stock. Discard the skin, bones, and cooked vegetables. If you have time, pour the stock into shallow pans and refrigerate 4 hours or longer, until fat is congealed and can be easily removed.

Otherwise, remove the fat with a baster or a cup made especially for the purpose.

Cut the cooked chicken into bite-size pieces.

Bring the defatted stock to a boil, and add the noodles. Simmer until the noodles are just slightly less tender than you desire. This will take 10–20 minutes, depending on the thickness of the noodles. While the noodles are cooking, sauté the sliced mushrooms in butter. Add the mushrooms and chicken to the pot when the noodles are almost ready. Allow the mixture to cook about 2 minutes longer, while you add salt and pepper to taste. Ladle chicken and noodles into bowls.

Making the noodles: mix the flour and salt in a large bowl. Make a well in the middle of the flour and add the eggs. Mix them in with your fingertips. Add the water and oil. Knead into a heavy dough. Divide the dough into 2 balls, wrap in plastic, and let sit for 1 hour. Knead the dough on a floured board. Roll out each ball to the thickness of pie crust, then roll it back into a ball and let it sit for about 30 minutes. Do this several times, rolling the dough a little thinner each time, and sprinkling the board with extra flour as needed. Finally, roll each ball out to be cut into noodles. The dough does not have to be paper-thin, but it can be no more than ¹⁄₁₆-inch thick. Cut the dough into noodles of a width and length of your choosing. Let the noodles air dry for at least 2 hours, or all day.

NOODLES

2 cups all-purpose flour
¼ tsp. salt
3 eggs
2 tbsp. water
1 tsp. vegetable oil

Stuffed Chicken Thighs

MAKES 4 SERVINGS

1 tbsp. olive oil

¼ cup chopped onion

¼ cup chopped celery

about 5 oz. uncooked chicken
   livers, finely chopped

¼ tsp. ground ginger

¼ tsp. salt

dash of pepper

2 cups soft breadcrumbs

1 tart green apple, peeled, cored
   and cut into ¼-inch dice

½ cup coarsely chopped walnuts

4–5 tbsp. melted butter

about 3 tbsp. milk

8 chicken thighs

½ tsp. paprika

Tart apple, walnuts, ginger, celery, and liver make a tasty melange of flavors and textures. The liver is not enough to dominate the stuffing, and it is nicely complemented by the other flavors. This stuffing is a little messy, since there's not enough bread for it to clump together, but that's what allows the other ingredients to assert themselves. Put any leftover stuffing in a small, lightly buttered casserole or baking dish, and add a little melted butter or milk to keep it moist. Cover the dish and bake it during the last 20 minutes while the chicken is cooking, then serve it on the side.

In a medium skillet, sauté the onion and celery in the olive oil for 3 minutes. Add the chopped liver. Cook, stirring frequently, until liver is thoroughly browned, about 5 minutes. Add ginger, salt, and pepper, and mix well.

In a medium bowl, mix breadcrumbs, apple, and walnuts. Add the liver mixture. Add 2 tbsp. melted butter and enough milk so that stuffing is thoroughly moistened but not mushy.

Preheat oven to 350°F. Lightly grease a shallow 9 × 9-inch (or slightly larger) baking dish. Trim excess skin and fat from chicken thighs. Remove bone by cutting thighs almost in half along the bone. Cut out the bone with a sharp knife. Place the boned thighs skin side down and spread out so you have a flat rectangle of meat. Place about 2 tbsp. of stuffing along the center of each thigh. Roll up and fasten with wooden toothpicks, or tie with string. Push any spilled stuffing back into roll and place in baking pan, rolled edges up.

Mix 2–3 tbsp. melted butter and paprika. Brush butter over thighs. Lightly sprinkle with salt, if desired. Bake at 350°F, occasionally basting with pan juices, until chicken is cooked through, 50–60 minutes.

Chicken Pot Pie with Cornmeal Crust

MAKES 6 SERVINGS

5 tbsp. butter, divided

1 small onion, chopped

3 cups sliced mushrooms

4 tbsp. flour

1½ cups chicken stock

½ cup heavy cream

1 tsp. salt

¼ tsp. pepper

pinch of cayenne

3 cups cubed cooked chicken

crust (recipe follows)

This version of old-fashioned chicken pot pie is made with a comforting mixture of chicken and mushrooms as its main ingredients. If you prefer, you can substitute peas and carrots for part of the mushrooms. Some people also like to add a little diced ham to the filling.

Sauté the onion and mushrooms in 1 tbsp. butter for 6–8 minutes, until the mushrooms are very tender. In a small saucepan, make a light roux of the remaining 4 tbsp. butter and flour. Heat but do not brown the butter, then add the flour. Cook over low heat, stirring constantly, until the roux is a tan color. While the roux is cooking, bring the chicken stock to a boil. When the roux is done, add a little of the stock to the roux, then gradually stir in the rest. Add the cream, the mushrooms, seasonings, and the chicken. Mix well. Pour into a 10-inch deep-dish pie dish.

To make the crust, preheat oven to 425°F.

Mix the flour, cornmeal, sugar, baking powder, and salt in a medium bowl. In a small bowl, combine the egg, milk, and melted butter. Pour the liquid ingredients into the dry ingredients, and stir until the flour is evenly moistened. Spoon the batter over the top of the chicken filling.

Bake until the crust is golden brown, about 40 minutes.

CRUST

1 cup flour

1 cup cornmeal

1 tbsp. sugar

1 tbsp. baking powder

1 tsp. salt

1 egg, lightly beaten with fork

1 cup milk

4 tbsp. melted butter

Roast Pork with Rhubarb Sauce

RHUBARB SAUCE

3 cups diced fresh rhubarb (about 1½ lb.)

1 large tart green apple, peeled, cored, and diced

⅓ cup sugar

½ tsp. grated orange peel

½ tsp. allspice

⅛ tsp. black pepper

This is an elegant but simple way to serve pork. The meat is flavored with garlic and rubbed with a mix of spices before roasting. It is served with an easy-to-make rhubarb sauce.

Preheat oven to 350°F.

Trim the loin of all excess fat, leaving no more than ⅛-inch layer of fat. Cut deep, narrow slits all over the surface of the meat and insert slivers of garlic. Mix the spices, then rub all over the pork. Roll up the meat like a jelly roll, and tie it with string if it is not already tied. Place the meat on a rack in a roasting pan. Roast for about 35–40 minutes a pound, until a thermometer inserted into the thickest part of the meat registers at least 140°F, and up to 170°F if you want the pork well-done. Let the meat sit for about

15 minutes before carving into slices ½–1-inch thick. Serve with rhubarb sauce on the side.

To make rhubarb sauce buy slim, crisp stalks of rhubarb. Trim off all leaves and roots. If the rhubarb seems tough and stringy, peel off the stringy parts. But try to avoid this by buying younger, tender stalks because the outer layer contains much of the color and flavor.

Put all ingredients in medium saucepan with 2 tbsp. water to avoid scorching. The rhubarb will put out a lot of liquid as it cooks. Simmer over low heat until apples are tender but not mushy, about 10 minutes. Taste and adjust the sugar if necessary; the sauce should not be too sweet, but neither should it be so tart that your lips pucker. Sauce may be served hot or cold.

MAKES 4–6 SERVINGS

2-lb. boneless pork loin

4 cloves garlic, peeled and cut into slivers

1 tsp. salt

½ tsp. freshly ground pepper

½ tsp. dry mustard

½ tsp. allspice

½ tsp. cloves

½ tsp. dried thyme leaves

Rhubarb sauce (recipe follows)

Pork Chops in Mustard Gravy

MAKES 4 SERVINGS

¼ cup olive oil

2 tbsp. fresh lime juice

1 tsp. Dijon-style mustard

1½ tsp. each chopped fresh sage,
rosemary, and oregano (or
½ tsp. dried herbs)

4 thick-cut pork chops

salt and pepper

1–2 tbsp. olive oil

¼ cup dry white wine

¼ cup beef stock or water

1 tbsp. flour

¼ cup milk or heavy cream

1 tbsp. Dijon-style mustard

1 tsp. chopped fresh rosemary (or
½ tsp. dried)

¼ tsp. salt

pepper

Pork chops are marinated in oil and vinegar laced with fresh herbs, browned, then baked in the same pan. A delicious gravy spiked with mustard and rosemary is made from the drippings. If you put the pork chops in the marinade in the morning, they will be well-seasoned by dinner time.

Make a marinade of the olive oil, lime juice, mustard and herbs. Put chops in a glass or other non-reactive shallow dish. Pour marinade over them. Turn the chops and spoon marinade over them so they are completely coated. Let them sit, refrigerated, at least 4 hours.

Preheat the oven to 350°F. Remove the chops from the marinade, and lightly salt and pepper them. Use a skillet or flame-proof casserole dish that is large enough for all the chops, and which can be used both on the stovetop and in the oven. Heat just enough oil that the pan is thinly coated. Brown the chops briefly on both sides. Pour the marinade over the chops.

Bake the chops, covered, until they are cooked through, about 1 hour.

Remove the chops from the pan and keep them warm in the oven. Remove excess fat from the pan with a baster, or pour the pan juices into a heatproof glass container, submerge it in cold water, and spoon off the fat that rises to the top. Then return the juices to the pan.

Add wine to the pan. Over medium-high heat, deglaze the pan, stirring and scraping browned bits off the bottom. Cook until the juices are reduced by half. Add ¼ cup beef stock or water, and stir well. In a small cup, mix flour with 1 tbsp. cream or milk, and stir to a smooth, thick paste. Stir in remaining milk or cream. Add the cream to the pan and whisk it in. Add the mustard, rosemary, salt, and pepper. Stir until smooth, adding a little milk or stock if it is too thick, or flour mixed with a little milk if it is too thin. Spoon the gravy over the chops, or serve it on the side.

Chicken and Shrimp Pilau

MAKES 6 SERVINGS

2 half chicken breasts, cubed
1 tsp. salt, divided
¼ tsp. black pepper
¼ tsp. cayenne
½ tsp. dried thyme
1 tsp. paprika
3 cups chicken broth
2 tbsp. chopped fresh parsley
1½ cups rice
3 strips bacon
3 stalks celery, diced
2 cups chopped onion
1 cup chopped green pepper
2 cloves garlic, minced
olive oil, if needed
½ lb. medium shrimp, peeled and deveined
few drops Tabasco sauce

Pilau – also spelled perloo and purloo – comes from the Carolinas, and is a cousin to New Orleans jambalaya. It is a rice dish cooked with vegetables and meat, although the quantity of meat varies greatly. Some recipes call for just a little meat as seasoning, and make pilau a side dish. This pilau is a main dish.

Mix ½ tsp. salt with the black pepper, cayenne, thyme, and paprika. Sprinkle it over the chicken cubes, and toss to spread the spices evenly. Put the chicken in the refrigerator, and let it absorb the spices while you are preparing the other ingredients.

Bring the chicken broth, remaining ½ tsp. salt, and the parsley to a boil. Add the rice. Cover and lower heat. Cook until rice is tender and liquid is absorbed, about 25 minutes.

Fry the bacon in a very large skillet or dutch oven. When it is crisp, remove the bacon and crumble it. Saute the onion, celery, green pepper, and garlic in the bacon fat until vegetables are limp, about 5 minutes. Remove the vegetables with a slotted spoon and set aside.

Add a little olive oil to the pan, if necessary, and saute the chicken cubes until they are browned and cooked through, 8–10 minutes. Remove the chicken and set aside.

Again, add a little olive oil to the pan if it's needed. Saute the shrimp until they turn white-pink and curl tightly, 3–4 minutes. Return the chicken and vegetables to the pan, and add the cooked rice, bacon crumbles, and Tabasco sauce. Mix well, taste, and add Tabasco, salt, and pepper as needed.

★ *ABOVE Florida's Everglades once stretched across a hundred miles of southern Florida, but have shrunk after more than a century of dredging and draining. The great swamp is home to an exotic mix of wildlife and plants, and is visited by millions of tourists each year.*

Rabbit in Mushroom-Wine Sauce

MAKES 2-3 SERVINGS

1 rabbit, about 3 lb., cut into
*   pieces*
⅓ cup plus 3 tbsp. flour
¼ tsp. salt
dash of pepper
3 garlic cloves, peeled and
*   crushed*
2 tbsp. olive oil
2 tbsp. butter
1 cup chicken stock
1 cup dry, full-bodied red wine
3 tsp. fresh tarragon, divided
3 tbsp. butter
½ lb. mushrooms, sliced
1 clove garlic, minced
¼ cup sour cream
¼ cup milk
salt and pepper to taste

Don't be put off by the lavender tinge that wine brings to this sauce. Wine, mushrooms, and fresh tarragon combine to make a delicious gravy. Be sure to use fresh tarragon, as the dried herb loses most of the essential flavor. This recipe also works well with chicken.

Mix ⅓ cup flour, salt, and pepper. Dredge the rabbit pieces in the flour mixture, and shake off any excess.

In a large, deep skillet, or Dutch oven, heat 2 tbsp. each of olive oil and butter, and sauté the 3 cloves of garlic until they are lightly browned. Press each piece of garlic to squeeze out the juices, remove cloves from the pan, and discard. Add the rabbit pieces to the pan and cook until golden brown on each side. The pieces should not be cooked through.

Add the chicken stock, wine, and 2 tsp. fresh tarragon to the rabbit. Bring to a slight boil, then cover and reduce heat.

Cook over low heat, turning once or twice, until the rabbit is tender, 45 minutes to 1 hour. Check occasionally to make sure the liquid does not dry out.

While the rabbit is cooking, sauté the mushrooms, minced garlic and 1 tsp. fresh tarragon in 3 tbsp. butter for about 10 minutes. Set aside.

When the rabbit is done, remove it from the pan and put it in the oven to keep it warm. Discard all but 1 cup of liquid from the pan, or add a little chicken stock if needed to bring up to this amount. Mix ¼ cup of the juices with 3 tbsp. flour until it is a smooth paste. Add the flour mixture to the rest of the pan juices, whisk until smooth, and cook until it bubbles. Add sour cream and milk, and whisk again until sauce is smooth. Let it heat slightly, but don't let it boil. Stir in the sautéed mushrooms. To serve, spoon the sauce over the rabbit pieces.

★ *ABOVE The Appalachian Mountains cut across Walker County in the far northwestern corner of Georgia.*

DESSERTS

Rhubarb custard pie

Buttermilk pie with raspberry sauce

Caramel apple pie

Chocolate raspberry pie

Jeanie's sheet cake

Coconut cake

Williamsburg cake

Lemon-chocolate chess pie

Sour cream peach pie

Pecan squares

Coconut cream pie

Boiled cookies

Ginger pear cobbler

Strawberries in meringue nests

Kentucky jam cake

Pumpkin cheesecake

Peach cranberry turnovers

★ *OPPOSITE The magnolia, with its large, creamy white blooms and sweet perfume, is the state flower of Louisiana, where it grows in abundance.*

Rhubarb Custard Pie

MAKES 6–8 SERVINGS

9-inch pie crust, pre-baked

FILLING

4 cups diced rhubarb
1/2 cup sugar
1 tsp. grated lemon peel
1/4 tsp. cinnamon
1/4 tsp. ginger
2 tbsp. flour

CUSTARD

1 cup heavy cream
2 eggs, lightly beaten
1/2 cup sugar
1 tsp. vanilla
1/4 tsp. cinnamon
1/4 tsp. ginger

The appearance of rhubarb in the grocery store used to mean spring had arrived, but now it's hothouse-grown and available year-round. Rhubarb is full of good flavor, but, even more than cranberries, needs a liberal addition of sugar to turn its overwhelming sourness into a pleasing tartness. That's one reason why the filling for this pie is briefly simmered with sugar before it's poured into the crust and baked. The result is an ideal pie filling, which is why rhubarb was long known as the pie plant. Look for slender, crisp stalks of rhubarb. Trim off all leaves and roots, which are poisonous. If the stalk seems particularly tough and stringy, peel it, but try to avoid buying tough stalks because that red outer layer is where the color and much of the flavor are concentrated.

Preheat oven to 350°F.

Put the rhubarb, sugar, lemon peel, and spices into a saucepan. Add 2 tbsp. water to keep it from scorching. Rhubarb contains a lot of water and will produce plenty of juice once it's started. Simmer the rhubarb over a low fire, just until rhubarb is tender, 5–10 minutes. Add the flour, which will thicken some of the juices. Set aside.

Mix all custard ingredients. Pour the rhubarb into the pie crust, and pour the custard over it. Bake at 350°F until custard turns golden brown, 40–50 minutes.

Buttermilk Pie with Raspberry Sauce

MAKES 6–8 SERVINGS

8-inch or 9-inch pre-baked pie
    crust
1 cup sugar
1/2 cup butter at room
    temperature
2 eggs, separated
1 cup buttermilk
1 tsp. vanilla
1/2 tsp. nutmeg
3 tbsp. flour
raspberry sauce (recipe follows)

This is a very simple, old-fashioned pie with a custardy, subtly-flavored filling. It's delicious plain, but the easy raspberry sauce provides a tart and colorful contrast.

Preheat oven to 350°F.

Cream butter and sugar. Add egg yolks, buttermilk, vanilla, nutmeg, and flour. Mix well. In a separate bowl, whip egg whites until soft peaks form. Gently fold the egg whites into the buttermilk filling. Pour the filling into the pie crust. Bake until custard is set and top is golden brown, about 40 minutes. Custard will set a little more as it cools. To serve, spoon raspberry sauce over individual slices.

To make the sauce, put the berries in a small pan with 1 tbsp. water to prevent scorching. Add sugar. (Note: If you are using frozen berries that already have sugar or sweet syrup added, reduce or eliminate the extra sugar, depending on your taste.) Cook until the mixture bubbles, then reduce heat and simmer 5 minutes. Crush some of the berries with the back of a fork or spoon. Let sauce cool.

RASPBERRY SAUCE

2 cups raspberries, fresh or frozen
1/3 cup sugar

Caramel Apple Pie

MAKES 6–8 SERVINGS

Pastry for a 2-crust, 9-inch pie

FILLING

4 cups apples, peeled, cored, and
    sliced
1/4 cup brown sugar
1 tsp. cinnamon
1/4 tsp. nutmeg
2 tbsp. plus 2 tsp. flour

A mixture of brown sugar, cream, and butter gives this apple pie a lovely caramel flavor. Use a tart green apple, such as Pippin or Granny Smith.

Preheat oven to 375°F.

Roll out half the pastry for the bottom crust and fit it into a 9-inch pie pan. Roll out the top crust and set it aside.

Make the filling by tossing the sliced apples with the brown sugar, cinnamon, nutmeg, and 2 tbsp. flour. Sprinkle the remaining 2 tsp. flour over the bottom of the unbaked pie shell. Set aside.

To make the caramel sauce, mix the brown sugar, half and half, butter, and vanilla in a small saucepan. Heat, stirring almost constantly, until the butter is melted, the sugar is dissolved, and the sauce is smooth.

Put the apple filling in the pie shell. Pour the caramel sauce over it. Cover with the top crust, seal the two crusts together, and crimp the edges. Cut a few vents in the top of the crust. Bake at 375°F until the crust is lightly browned, 45–50 minutes.

CARAMEL

2/3 cup brown sugar
1/4 cup half and half
4 tbsp. butter
1 tsp. vanilla

Chocolate Raspberry Pie

MAKES 6–8 SERVINGS

9-inch pie shell, unbaked

FILLING

3 cups raspberries

2/3 cup sugar

3 tbsp. flour

2 tsp. fresh lemon juice

CREAM

2 tsp. (1 envelope) unflavored gelatin

3 tbsp. cold water

1 3/4 cups heavy cream, divided

1/3 cup powdered sugar

1 tsp. vanilla

This pie combines three favorites — raspberries, whipped cream, and chocolate — to make a spectacular dessert. It begins as a simple raspberry pie, cooked like other fruit pies. But instead of a top crust, the cooled pie is covered with a thick layer of whipped cream, then coated with a thin layer of chocolate. None of the steps is difficult, but the pie needs time to cool or set between each step, so it must be started the night before or early in the day you plan to serve it. You may use a standard pastry pie crust or a chocolate crumb crust. Note: If you are using frozen berries, measure them after they have thawed. Also, if the raspberries were frozen in a sugar syrup, decrease the amount of sugar, depending on the sweetness of the berries.

Preheat oven to 350°F.

To make the filling, combine raspberries, sugar, flour, and lemon juice. Mix gently. Pour into pie crust. Bake 50 minutes at 350°F. Let pie cool completely before proceeding.

Put 3 tbsp. water in a small glass cup or bowl. Sprinkle gelatin over the water. Place the bowl in shallow hot water in a small pan over low heat. Let it stand until the gelatin is dissolved.

Pour 1 1/2 cups of the cream into a large bowl with the powdered sugar and vanilla. Beat the cream until it barely starts to thicken. Stir the reserved 1/4 cup cream into the dissolved gelatin, then pour it back into the partially whipped cream. Immediately resume beating until the cream holds soft peaks. Spread the cream over the top of the raspberries, smoothing out any peaks. Refrigerate the pie until the cream has set — at least 1 hour — before proceeding. The gelatin allows the cream to hold its shape when you put the chocolate glaze on it.

To make the glaze, put the chocolate, shortening, cream, and sugar in the top of a double boiler over gently simmering water. Stir until the chocolate is melted and the sugar is dissolved, then whisk until the mixture is smooth. Remove the chocolate from the heat and let it cool to room temperature, then whisk it again.

Gently spoon a little of the chocolate onto the whipped cream and spread it thinly. Continue spooning and spreading the chocolate until the entire surface of the pie is covered with a thin chocolate glaze. Return the pie to the refrigerator and let the chocolate harden — at least 30 minutes — before serving.

GLAZE

4 oz. semi-sweet chocolate

1 tbsp. Crisco-type shortening (not butter or margarine)

3 tbsp. heavy cream

2 tbsp. sugar

Jeanie's Sheet Cake

MAKES 8–10 SERVINGS

1½ cups all-purpose flour

¾ tsp. baking soda

½ tsp. salt

3 tbsp. unsweetened cocoa

¾ cup butter at room
   temperature

1½ cups sugar

2 eggs

½ cup buttermilk

2 tsp. powdered espresso or
   instant coffee

¼ cup hot water

1 tsp. vanilla

6 oz. semi-sweet chocolate chips

A number of states claim this chocolate sheet cake. I'll just attribute it to my friend Jeanie, who introduced me to a variation on this cake and swore that if I made it for our colleagues, it would get wolfed down in seconds. She was right. It's an easy-to-make cake, dense and rich, somewhere between cake and brownies, with a thick and gooey frosting.

Preheat oven to 400°F. Lightly grease a 9 × 13-inch cake pan, and dust it with unsweetened cocoa.

Sift together the flour, baking soda, salt, and cocoa. In a large bowl, cream the butter and sugar. Beat in the eggs. Alternately add the dry ingredients and the buttermilk to the butter mixture, beating with each addition. Dissolve the coffee in the hot water, and add it to the batter. Add the vanilla. Stir in the chocolate chips.

Pour into the greased pan, and bake at 400°F until a knife inserted in the center of the cake comes out clean, 20–25 minutes.

While the cake is baking, make the frosting. The cake should be frosted while still warm.

Bring the butter, cocoa and milk to a boil in a medium saucepan. Remove from heat and add the vanilla and sugar, stirring until smooth. Stir in the walnuts. Spread frosting on the cake while the cake is still warm.

FROSTING

½ cup butter

¼ cup unsweetened cocoa

6 tbsp. milk

1 tsp. vanilla

3½ cups powdered sugar
   (approximately a 1-lb. box)

¾ cup chopped walnuts

★ 129 ★

Coconut Cake

MAKES 8–12 SERVINGS

2 cups all-purpose flour
1 tbsp. baking powder
1/2 tsp. salt
1 1/4 cups sugar
1/2 cup butter, at room
    temperature
1 cup milk
1 tsp. vanilla
2 cups coconut, shredded or
    flaked
4 egg whites

LEMON FILLING

2 egg yolks
1/2 cup sugar
2 tsp. finely grated lemon peel
2 tbsp. fresh lemon juice
pinch of salt
1/3 cup heavy cream
1 tbsp. butter

A thick lemon custard is hidden between the layers of this white cake, which is then covered with a pure white icing and sprinkled with coconut. It is a beautiful cake, and it tastes even better.

Preheat oven to 350°F. Grease and flour two 9-inch round cake pans.

Sift together the flour, baking powder, and salt. In a large bowl, cream the butter and sugar. Add the vanilla to the milk, then add it alternately with the flour to the butter-sugar mixture. Stir in the coconut.

In a separate bowl, beat the egg whites until stiff peaks form. Gently fold the whites into the batter. Pour the batter into the cake pans. Bake the cakes at 350°F until a knife inserted in the center comes out clean, about 25 minutes. Let the layers cool completely before filling and icing them.

To make the lemon filling combine all ingredients except butter in the top of a double boiler, over simmering water. Stir constantly until the custard thickens, 8–10 minutes. Remove from heat and beat in the butter. Let the custard cool. Place the bottom layer of the cake on a platter, with the top side down. When the custard is cool, spread it on the bottom layer of the cake. Place the upper layer on top of the custard, right side up.

For the frosting combine all ingredients except vanilla and coconut in the top of a double boiler, over rapidly boiling water. Beat them constantly with a hand-held beater for 7 minutes, until icing holds soft peaks. Remove it from the heat and beat in the vanilla. Continue beating, if necessary, until the icing is right for spreading.

Spread the icing across the top and down the sides of the cake. Sprinkle coconut over the top, and gently press it into the sides.

FROSTING

1 1/2 cups sugar
1/4 cup water
2 tbsp. light corn syrup
3 egg whites
1/4 tsp. cream of tartar
1 tsp. vanilla
1–1 1/2 cups coconut, shredded or
    flaked

Williamsburg Cake

MAKES 6–10 SERVINGS

2 1/2 cups all-purpose flour
1 1/2 tsp. baking soda
1/2 tsp. salt
3/4 cup butter, at room
    temperature
1 1/2 cups sugar
3 eggs
1 1/2 tsp. vanilla
finely grated zest of 1 orange
1 cup buttermilk
1/2 cup orange juice
1 cup golden raisins
1/2 cup chopped pecans

This orange layer cake traces its roots to colonial Virginia. The tall cake is full of pecans and golden raisins, and iced with an easy but delicious orange frosting. As a teenager, this was the first cake I baked from scratch and it was immediately one of my favorites.

Preheat oven to 350°F. Grease and flour three 8-inch round cake pans.

Sift together the flour, baking soda, and salt. In a large bowl, cream the butter and sugar. Beat in the eggs, vanilla, and orange zest into the butter mixture. Add the flour alternately with the buttermilk and orange juice. Stir in the raisins and pecans. Pour the batter into the cake pans. Bake at 350°F until a knife inserted in the center comes out clean, about 30 minutes. Let the cake cool completely before frosting it.

To make the frosting, cream butter and sugar. Add orange juice or liqueur until frosting is smooth and spreadable but not runny. Stir in orange zest.

Note: This frosting will cover all three layers and sides, but if you believe that a cake's sole purpose is to support the frosting, you may want to increase the amount of the recipe.

FROSTING

4 1/2 cups powdered sugar
10 tbsp. butter at room
    temperature
4–5 tbsp. orange liqueur or
    orange juice
2 tbsp. finely grated orange zest

Coconut Cake

Lemon-Chocolate Chess Pie

MAKES 6–8 SERVINGS

9-inch pie shell, pre-baked
2 oz. semi-sweet chocolate
1½ cups sugar
½ cup butter at room
    temperature
4 eggs
¾ cup milk
2 tbsp. cornmeal
¼ cup fresh lemon juice
grated rind of 2 lemons

A cousin to the buttermilk pie, the chess pie is another traditional Southern dessert. Its name is believed to be a corruption of cheese, which is how the British once referred to egg custard. Here we've dressed up the basic chess pie with fresh lemon and a thin layer of chocolate hidden between the crust and the filling.

Melt the chocolate in a double boiler over simmering hot water. Spread it thinly on the bottom of the pre-baked crust. Allow chocolate to cool and harden before adding the filling.

Preheat oven to 375°F.

Cream sugar and butter. Beat in the eggs and milk until mixture is smooth. Add cornmeal, lemon juice and rind, and mix well. Pour into crust. Bake until custard sets and top is golden brown, about 50 minutes.

Sour Cream Peach Pie

If the South had an official fruit, it would be the peach. In this dessert, peaches are paired with a tangy sour cream sauce.

Preheat oven to 400°F. Arrange the peaches in the crust. (You can sprinkle a little flour over the crust first to keep it from getting soggy.) Mix remaining ingredients, except topping. Pour the sour cream mixture over the peaches. Bake the pie for 25 minutes at 400°F. While the pie is baking, make the topping.

Mix all the topping ingredients. After pie has cooked for 25 minutes, remove it from the oven and sprinkle the topping over it. Return pie to the oven and bake an additional 15 minutes.

MAKES 8 SERVINGS

unbaked pie crust for 9-inch tin
3 cups sliced and peeled peaches
¾ cup sour cream
1 egg, lightly beaten
½ tsp. vanilla
2 tbsp. flour
¼ tsp. salt
⅔ cup sugar

TOPPING

4 tbsp. flour
¼ cup brown sugar
1 tsp. cinnamon
¼ cup butter
⅓ cup chopped pecans or
    walnuts

★ *ABOVE Morgan City on the Atchafalaya River in southern Louisiana celebrates the pecan with its annual Pecan Festival. Louisiana orchards produce millions of pounds of pecans each year, some of which are used in such Louisiana favorites as pecan pie and pralines.*

Pecan Squares

MAKES 60-80 COOKIES

CRUST

1½ cups all-purpose flour

½ cup butter at room
    temperature

¾ cup brown sugar

½ tsp. vanilla

*These cookies are incredibly rich and sweet.
They are an irresistible finger-food
substitute for pecan pie. And they're easy
to make.*

Preheat oven to 350°F. Lightly butter
a 9 × 9-inch baking pan.

    Mix crust ingredients. Pat evenly into a
crust in the bottom of the pan. Bake at
350°F until golden, 16-20 minutes. Let
crust cool at least 10 minutes.

Put butter, sugar, and honey in medium
saucepan. Bring mixture to a boil, stirring
constantly. Add cream, return to just
barely boiling, and remove from heat. Add
vanilla and pecans. Pour over crust.

    Return cookies to oven. Cook until
mixture is bubbly and firm, about 30
minutes. Cool completely on a wire rack.
Cut into 1-1½-inch squares.

FILLING

½ cup butter

½ cup brown sugar

½ cup honey

3 tbsp. heavy cream

1 tsp. vanilla

2 cups pecan halves

Coconut Cream Pie

9-inch pie shell, pre-baked
½ cup sugar
4 tbsp. cornstarch
¼ tsp. salt
4 egg yolks
2½ cups milk, heated but not
   boiled
1 tsp. vanilla
1 tbsp. fresh lime juice
1½ tbsp. butter
1½ cups flaked coconut, divided
1 cup whipping cream
3 tbsp. powdered sugar

Lime juice adds a subtle tang to this rich custard filling, which is topped with whipped cream and coconut for an old-fashioned dessert.

Beat together the sugar, cornstarch, salt, and egg yolks for 1–2 minutes, until the mixture is pale yellow. Put the egg mixture in the top of a double boiler over simmering water. Add a little of the hot milk and whisk it in, then add the rest of the milk a little at a time, whisking constantly. Cook, stirring constantly, until the mixture thickens, about 10 minutes, depending on the temperature of the milk. Remove the custard from the heat. Stir in the vanilla, lime juice, butter, and 1 cup coconut. Pour the custard into the baked pie shell. Refrigerate at least 3 hours.

Whip the cream with the powdered sugar until soft peaks form. Gently spread the whipped cream over the pie. Sprinkle the remaining ½ cup coconut over the top.

Boiled Cookies

MAKES 3 DOZEN COOKIES

2 cups sugar

1/4 cup unsweetened cocoa

1/2 cup milk

1/2 cup butter

1/8 tsp. salt

2 cups oatmeal

1 cup shredded or flaked coconut

1/2 cup chopped pecans

2 tsp. vanilla

These chewy chocolate cookies are made on the stovetop without flour or eggs. They don't require any baking, although if you like a crisp cookie, you can bake them for about 8 minutes at 375°F. Some versions add peanut butter.

Put sugar, cocoa, milk, butter, and salt in a large saucepan. Bring the mixture to a boil, stirring frequently. Boil for 1½ minutes. Remove from heat. Stir in remaining ingredients.

Drop the dough by rounded tablespoons onto waxed paper. You need to work quickly before the mixture hardens, but be careful because the dough is very hot. Let cookies cool until they are set.

Ginger Pear Cobbler

CRUST

1¼ cups all-purpose flour

1/4 cup sugar

1½ tsp. baking powder

1/2 tsp. salt

1 tbsp. candied ginger, finely chopped

1/8 tsp. ground ginger

4 tbsp. shortening or butter, or a combination of the two

about 6 tbsp. milk

Everyone has a favorite recipe for peach cobbler, but here's one for pear cobbler, a sweet and underrated fruit that is available when peaches are out of season. Candied ginger, available in the spice section of most grocery stores, gives it an elegant touch.

Preheat oven to 375°F.

Toss pears with the sugar, cornstarch, and the candied and ground gingers. Place in a 5-cup casserole dish or oven-proof bowl.

To make the crust, mix dry ingredients and ginger. Work shortening in with two sharp knives or fingertips, until mixture resembles cornmeal. Add milk until dough loses its stiffness and gets a little sloppy. Pull out small handfuls of dough, pat into flat disks, and put on top of pears. Pinch the disks of dough together so they more or less form one solid crust.

Bake until top is golden brown, about 30 minutes.

MAKES 6 SERVINGS

FILLING

4 cups ripe pears (about 6), peeled, cored, and sliced

1/2 cup sugar

2 tbsp. cornstarch

2 tbsp. candied ginger, finely chopped

1/4 tsp. ground ginger

Boiled Cookies

Strawberries in Meringue Nests

MAKES 6 SERVINGS

6 meringue nests

4–5 cups of fresh strawberries, washed and hulled

orange custard sauce

MERINGUE NESTS

½ cup pecans

1 cup sugar, divided

4 egg whites (use the yolks in the custard sauce)

⅛ tsp. cream of tartar

1 tsp. vanilla

This luscious dessert consists of strawberries in a pecan-studded meringue shell, drizzled with a wonderful orange custard sauce. The nests and custard sauce can be prepared early in the day and assembled at dessert time. This recipe should not be made on a humid day, since the meringue nests will absorb the moisture and lose their crispness. If there's a dieter in the crowd, omit the custard sauce or substitute yogurt.

Preheat oven to 250°F. Line two baking sheets with waxed paper or parchment. On each sheet, draw three 5-inch circles. Lightly grease the paper within the circles.

In a food processor, process the pecans and ½ cup sugar until the pecans are finely ground. Set aside.

In a medium bowl, beat the egg whites and cream of tartar until they are foamy. Continue beating, adding the remaining sugar a tablespoon at a time, until stiff peaks form. Beat in the vanilla. Gently fold in the sugar-pecan mixture.

Using a rubber spatula, divide the meringue among the six circles. As much as possible, build up the circles around the edges. There won't be much more than a small rim.

Bake at 250°F, until meringue forms a crisp crust, 1–1½ hours. Meringue should not brown at all. Turn off the oven and leave the door open, but don't remove the meringues for at least 10 minutes. Then remove them and let them cool away from any drafts. When they are cool, carefully invert them onto a clean towel and gently peel off the waxed paper.

In a small pan, heat but do not boil the cream.

While the cream is warming, put egg yolks, sugar, and salt in the top of a double boiler over simmering water. Whisk ingredients together, and continue whisking or stirring. When cream is hot, pour it into the eggs, a little at a time, whisking constantly. Continue stirring until sauce thickens, 10 minutes or so, depending on how warm the cream was. When it thickens, whisk in the orange peel and liqueur. Let the custard cool, stirring occasionally. Refrigerate until serving time.

To assemble desserts, place one nest on each plate. Divide strawberries among the nests. Spoon custard over strawberries.

ORANGE CUSTARD SAUCE

1½ cups heavy cream

3 egg yolks

⅓ cup sugar

⅛ tsp. salt

2 tsp. grated orange peel

3 tbsp. orange liqueur

Kentucky Jam Cake

MAKES 6–12 SERVINGS

3 cups all-purpose flour

2 tsp. baking powder

1 tsp. baking soda

1/2 tsp. salt

1 1/2 tsp. cinnamon

1/2 tsp. cloves

1 tsp. nutmeg

1/2 tsp. allspice

1 cup butter, at room temperature

1 1/2 cups brown sugar

4 eggs, separated

1 cup buttermilk

1 cup raspberry or blackberry jam

3/4 cup coarsely chopped pecans or walnuts

Jam cake, a favorite in Kentucky and Tennessee, is a rich spice cake with berry jam stirred in. It will fill your kitchen with a delicious smell of spice and warm jam. The caramel frosting, cooked much like fudge, is luscious.

Preheat oven to 350°F. Grease and flour two 9-inch cake pans.

Sift dry ingredients together. In a separate, large bowl, cream the butter and brown sugar. Add the egg yolks to the creamed mixture. Alternately add the dry ingredients and the buttermilk to the mixture, about one-third of each at a time, until the batter is well-mixed. Stir in the jam and nuts.

In a separate bowl, beat the egg whites until they form soft peaks. Gently fold the beaten whites into the batter. Divide batter between the two 9-inch pans. Bake at 350°F 40–45 minutes, until a knife inserted in the center comes out clean.

Let the layers cool about 10 minutes before turning them out onto cake racks. Let them cool completely before frosting.

Before you begin cooking the frosting, prepare the cake. If the tops of the layers are too high and rounded, slice off the top. Brush off any excess crumbs. Place the bottom cake layer, top side down, on a flat work surface. If you are using the serving platter, place overlapping strips of wax paper or foil around and under the edge of the cake. When the frosting has set, you'll remove these strips of paper and the drips of frosting.

For the caramel frosting you'll need a candy thermometer for this candy-like frosting. When it is done, you must frost the cake immediately.

Cook brown sugar, cream, and corn syrup in a heavy, medium saucepan. Stir until the and sugar is dissolved. Cover the pan and let the mixture continue cooking for 3 minutes, until the steam has washed down any sugar crystals on the side of the pan. Remove the cover and continue cooking without stirring, until the frosting reaches the soft ball stage, 238°F. Remove from heat, add the butter, and stir until it is well incorporated. Add the vanilla. Beat the icing by hand until it is thick and creamy but has not lost its gloss, 5–10 minutes. If it becomes too heavy, thin it with a little cream.

Working quickly, frost the top of the bottom layer. Place the second layer, top side up, on top of the frosted layer. Frost the top of the cake, then the sides. The frosting probably will droop a little on the sides. After the frosting sets, you can trim it off when you remove the paper strips or move the cake to a serving platter.

CARAMEL FROSTING

2 1/2 cups brown sugar

1 cup heavy cream (not half and half)

1 tbsp. light corn syrup

4 tbsp. butter

1 tsp. vanilla

Pumpkin Cheesecake

MAKES 8–10 SERVINGS

CRUST

1½ cups gingersnap crumbs

½ cup pecans

2 tbsp. sugar

⅓ cup melted butter

If you like pumpkin pie, you'll love this rich and creamy pumpkin cheesecake. It's baked in a crust of gingersnap crumbs, and lightly spiced for a delicious dessert. The cheesecake is easy to make, and can be baked a day in advance. If you buy canned pumpkin, make sure it's pure pumpkin, not sweetened and spiced pumpkin pie filling.

Preheat oven to 350°F.

Note: The gingersnap crumbs are measured after they are ground into crumbs. The pecans are measured before they are ground.

To make the crust, grind the pecans and mix them with the gingersnap crumbs and sugar. This step is easiest if you process them together in the food processor. Mix in the melted butter. Pour the crumb mixture into an ungreased 10-inch springform pan. Press the crumbs into a crust across the bottom and an inch or so up the sides of the pan. Bake 8–10 minutes at 350°F. Let the crust cool.

Set oven at 325°F.

To make the filling, cream the cream cheese and sugar. Add the pumpkin and sour cream, and mix well. Beat in the eggs one at a time. Mix in the seasonings. Pour the filling into the cooled crust. Bake until the filling is set in the center, about 1 hour and 10 minutes.

FILLING

1½ lb. cream cheese at room temperature

1 cup sugar

1½ cups cooked pumpkin

1 cup sour cream

4 eggs

1 tsp. cinnamon

½ tsp. ground ginger

¼ tsp. ground cloves

Peach-Cranberry Turnovers

MAKES ABOUT 14 TURNOVERS

2 cups plus 2 tbsp. all-purpose
*   flour*

1 tsp. salt

¾ cup solid shortening

¼ cup butter

4–5 tbsp. cold water

2 cups peaches, peeled and cut
*   into ¼-inch to ½-inch chunks*

½ cup cranberries, coarsely
*   chopped*

⅔ cup sugar

pinch of salt

2 tbsp. cream

additional sugar for tops

Sweet peaches complement tart cranberries in these turnovers, which make excellent finger food for a picnic or a stand-up party.

Make crust. Mix 2 cups flour with salt, then cut in butter. Mix in water until dough clings to itself but is not wet. The dough will be easier to handle if you refrigerate it at least one hour, then remove it from the refrigerator and bring it back to room temperature – about an hour – before rolling it out.

In the meantime, make filling. Combine peaches, cranberries, sugar, salt and remaining 2 tbsp. flour.

Preheat oven to 425°F. Lightly oil two baking sheets.

Roll about half the dough to a thickness of ⅛-inch. Cut out circles of 4½ inches. Pick up scraps, combine with remaining dough, and roll out. Continue rolling and making circles until you've used up the dough.

Place about 2 tbsp. peach filling in the center of each circle. Fold top over, so it forms a crescent. Pinch edges together all the way around. Moisten your fingers if necessary to be sure the edges are sealed, otherwise all the juices will run out during baking.

Brush the tops with cream, then sprinkle with sugar. Place them on baking sheets. Bake at 425°F until turnovers are lightly browned, about 25 minutes.

★ **ABOVE** *Peaches, the official state fruit of South Carolina,*
are grown throughout the South.

INDEX